OCCUPYING WALL STREET

OCCUPYING WALL STREET

The Inside Story of an Action that Changed America

Writers for the 99%

OR BOOKS
New York • London

© 2011 Writers for the 99%.

Published by OR Books, New York and London.
Visit our website at www.orbooks.com

First printing 2011.

Cataloging-in-Publication data is available from the Library of Congress
A catalog record for this book is available from the British Library.

ISBN 978-1-935928-68-3 paperback
ISBN 978-1-935928-64-5 e-book

Typeset by Wordstop Technologies, Chennai, India

Printed by BookMobile in the United States and CPI Books Ltd in the United Kingdom.
The U.S. printed edition of this book comes on Forest Stewardship Council-certified,
30% recycled paper. The printer, BookMobile, is 100% wind-powered.

Contents

Zuccotti Park Occupied

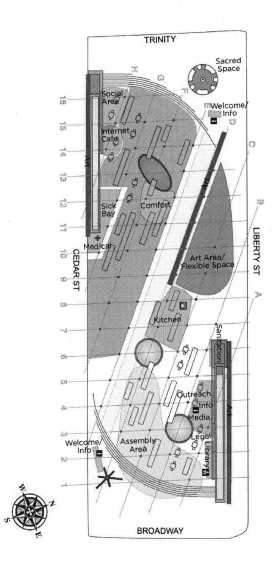

Introduction

This book is an account of the first months of the Occupy Wall Street movement (OWS). It is the result of a collaborative process that began a month after OWS had its first official action on September 17, 2011. Roughly sixty people—students and teachers, writers and artists, workers and professionals, female, male, people of color, white, old, young—have been involved in researching, writing, illustrating and editing the text. Although we make no claim to having produced an official or authorized narrative, many of us are active participants in OWS. All of us support the movement.

The idea of writing this book was first raised at a meeting of OWS's Education and Empowerment working group, held in the public atrium at 60 Wall Street, where many of the committees involved in the occupation meet. The suggestion was met with both interest and wariness. Some felt it was premature to attempt writing such a document. Others worried that the book would present itself, or be perceived as, an "official statement," despite reassurances from those working on it that they recognized claims to formal representation of a horizontal movement such as OWS to be both inappropriate and impossible.

At a subsequent meeting, the Education and Empowerment group voted against proceeding with the project. But those who remained enthusiastic about the idea decided to form their own group and to continue meeting independently. Members of this independent group still had several different and competing notions of what the book should be. Some saw it as a compilation of voices from the movement. Others envisioned an analysis of OWS's initial successes and failures. Still others wanted to write a handbook for future occupations. But all agreed that, as far as possible, the book should allow OWS to speak for itself.

To this end, dozens of interviews were conducted with a diverse range of people in and around the occupation. It is on this basis that we call this the "inside story" of the action. Interviewees, along with any other interested parties, were encouraged to attend the group's editorial meetings which were held at 60 Wall Street and were open to anyone who showed up. And we circulated the minutes of the meetings and the material we gathered to all who wanted to see it.

In the course of the project, participants generally tried to adopt OWS's method of decision-making—hand signs and all. This is not to say that we have always successfully adhered to the model set forth by the movement–our organization, like OWS, is an imperfect work in progress—but we have tried to observe its principles of direct democracy, consensus-based decision making, inclusiveness, and transparency.

As we go to press with this book, at the beginning of December 2011, many aspects of the future course of Occupy Wall Street remain unclear. But one thing is starkly evident: Under the banner "We are the 99%", the protest has given birth to America's most important progressive movement since the civil rights marches half a century ago. We hope, in the pages that follow, to tell the story of that beginning.

Beginnings

"Are you ready for a Tahrir moment?"
—*Call from* Adbusters, *July 13th 2011*

Occupy Wall Street is part of a global movement that has reached nearly every continent in the last year. Although the protests in disparate nations have taken place under different forms of government and have varied in the specificity of their demands, all have expressed a similar outrage with the inequities of unfettered global capitalism. In the first months of 2011, North Africa and the Middle East saw a myriad of popular protests. Unrest in Tunisia broke out on December 17, 2010, after a 26-year-old street vendor, Mohammed Bouazizi, lit himself ablaze because the police kept confiscating his wares to extort money, and he couldn't support his family of eight. Photos and videos of Bouazizi went viral on Facebook, igniting the rage of a generation of Tunisian youth and sparking colossal street demonstrations that led to the January 14 ouster of Tunisian president Ben Ali.

Next, protests erupted in Algeria, Lebanon, Jordan, Mauritania, Oman, and Saudi Arabia. The first Egyptian street protests took place on January 25, and by January 31, more than 250,000 had swarmed Cairo's Tahrir Square. In the mild winter weather, tens of thousands pitched small private tents and large open-air tents–canvas or transparent plastic sheets draped over beams. Visitors donated food to the "tent city," which brought together people of all ages, ideologies, and fashions. Popular committees were formed—a volunteer security service, trash collectors, medical services, a "Painters' Corner" for literate protesters to make signs, outdoor exhibitions of revolutionary banners, a makeshift stage for poets to recite their poems, even an open-air space for weddings. These committees and specially designated spaces would serve as a template for later movements in Europe and the United States.

Three days later, on February 14, the first wave of popular unrest in the U.S. shook the Wisconsin State Capitol in Madison and quickly reached nearby college campuses and the cities of Milwaukee, Green Bay, and Columbus, Ohio. The revolt had a specific target—the Wisconsin Budget Repair Bill, which also limited collective bargaining rights–but some protesters brandished Egyptian flags. On February 20, Egyptian union leader Kamal Abbas posted a YouTube video encouraging the "workers in Wisconsin." "We stand with you as you stood with us," he said.

By summer, the uprisings had spread to Sub-Saharan Africa, Latin America, Asia, and Europe. All of these protests influenced the people who were to participate in OWS. Senia, from OWS's Press Working Group, noted, for example, that Latina/o occupiers got "a really big inspiration" from less-publicized but recent protests in Chile, Colombia, Argentina, Brazil, Mexico, and Venezuela. But of all the protests of 2011, the massive Spanish encampments of *Los Indignados*, "the idignants," had perhaps the largest impact on the form and strategies of OWS.

Coordinated through Facebook and Twitter, the Spanish May 15 or 15M movement marched in roughly 60 Spanish cities and set up camps in highly visible public squares–giving the occupiers another name, *Las Acampadas, or* "camp-outs." Spain's public broadcasting company estimated that 6.5 to 8 million people joined the movement to protest welfare cuts, 20-percent unemployment, and other results of corporate greed.

Forming General Assemblies and working groups that reached decisions through a consensus-based process, the Indignados, even more than the Tahrir Square protesters, created structures that Occupy Wall Street would recycle and repurpose. Willie Osterweil, an activist involved in some of the earliest planning sessions for OWS, as well as the New York City General Assembly (NYCGA) and an earlier occupation called Bloombergsville, described the Spanish encampments he visited in June: "These camps became centers of information, protest, and revolutionary life: Indignados set up kitchens distributing free food, council booths focused on individual issues (the environment, the military, women's rights, etc.), and held meetings, teach-ins, and public discussions. This was a different kind of democracy, in which work, resources, and decisions are all shared. They cover the camps with placards displaying revolutionary slogans, and everywhere they go they leave behind cloth banners, cardboard signs, and graffiti."

The Spanish occupation electrified Willie. "In Spain, I gained renewed urgency and actually (rather than just intellectually) recognized the nature of the historical moment and the possibilities available to us here in the U.S.," he wrote in a blog. "The camp feels magical, but it's also totally jerry-rigged, improvisation built upon improvisation; tape, string, tarp, cloth, metal tent poles holding up a sagging canvas roof, plastic sheets propped up on three long bamboo rods taped together. A truly massive storm could take the whole thing down—but can't the same be said of the status quo? This camp, if joined by enough like it around the world, could be that storm."

During his visit, Willie built contacts with the Indignados and later conferred with them as he and other activists planned the occupations in New York City. "My experience in Spain was incredibly important in influencing my participation in Bloombergville, the NYCGA, and ultimately OWS." His interactions with the Indignados also show how organizers on different continents communicated and synced with each other, sharing ideas and tactics.

Among other commonalities, protesters across the world occupied spaces of symbolic importance and built an intentional community–attempting to create, in miniature, the kind of society that they wanted to live in–a society that took care of all its members' needs for food, clothing, shelter. The encampments gave them a sense of community and family, as well as a set location to talk to one anther and to the press. And while Facebook and Twitter were unevenly censored in some of these countries, many of the protesters carried smartphones–allowing highly organized movements to quickly mobilize massive numbers of people. This partly explains not only the wildfire spread of the 2011 protests but also their preference for non-hierarchical organizing and "horizontal" decision-making–which resembled online social networking, rather than traditional governing structures.

When Willie returned from Spain and the Indignados protests, the New Yorkers Against Budget Cuts (NYABC), the International Socialist Organization (ISO), and a few other groups were staging a much humbler occupation against Mayor Michael Bloomberg's proposed budget cuts. They had dubbed this three-week occupation Bloombergville. If the city council approved the mayor's proposal in its original form, 4,000 public school teachers would be laid off and 20 firehouses would close. Starting on June 16, several dozen protesters occupied the corner of Broadway and Park, near City Hall. The warm June nights made tents unnecessary, so the core group slept in sleeping bags under scaffolding. Major municipal and teacher's unions provided food, and the occupation also featured a small library and teach-ins by CUNY professors. The occupiers stayed until a few days after the June 29 city council approval of a modified budget.

Like the protesters who later took part in the early General Assemblies and Occupy Wall Street, the Bloombergville occupiers spoke of the strong sense of community they experienced through these occupations and meetings. The people who were there "forged very close and comradely relationships," said Jackie Di Salvo, 68, a Baruch professor and longtime labor organizer. "It was remarkably easy for me to sleep there. People stayed up all night to make sure everyone was okay." Jez Bold, 27, who joined Bloombergville in its second week, had long avoided more conventional forms of political protest, but he was "amazed by the idea of this community forming around this political act."

Jez explained that the sense of community came partly from the movement's atypical form: "It was not a protest or march in any traditional way. It certainly was not a rally in any traditional way. It was all these people who just planned to sleep there, so they all had to work together to sleep there." Jez watched Bloombergville inhabitants plan meals, create a library, lead teach-ins and even brainstorm a Bloombergville opera. These projects created an atmosphere Jez described as "sort of like a porch. Like everybody had a porch in New York and you could go down and hang out on your collective porch on Park Place and Broadway. "

Jez also witnessed the arrests of the "Bloombergville 13," who ziptied themselves together in the lobby to prevent the city council from voting on the budget deal. "They all sat down, ziptied their arms together and sat down in a circle and refused to leave. Police came in, told them to leave, they refused," Jez recalled. "They started cutting off zipties, someone re-ziptied themselves to each other, and eventually just pulled them off one by on and took them into the back," arresting all of them. The following day, the city council voted. "Everyone was pretty disappointed," he said, when they learned that a large budget cut had been approved. But some took heart from the fact that the city council had modified Bloomberg's proposal and deleted most of the layoffs and firehouse closures.

* * *

The NYABC had just finished the Bloombergville occupation when, on July 13, the Vancouver-based, ecological, anti-consumerist magazine *Adbusters* released its call to action:

#OCCUPY WALL STREET

Are you ready for a Tahrir moment?
On Sept 17, flood into lower Manhattan, set up tents, kitchens, peaceful barricades and occupy Wall Street.

On the magazine's Web site, a blog post below the ad urged its readers to catch the *Zeitgeist* and fashion themselves into a movement that was "a fusion of Tahrir with the acampadas of Spain." The post's author envisioned a crowd of 20,000 descending on Wall Street "for a few months," in order to "incessantly repeat one simple demand in a plurality of voices." For a movement that would later be lambasted for lacking clear demands, it's ironic that the blog post suggested that the occupation should revolve around just one: "we demand that Barack Obama ordain a Presidential Commission tasked with ending the influence money has over our representatives in Washington."

Adbusters gave Occupy Wall Street a name, assignment, and due date–along with a nudge to model itself on the Egyptian and Spanish encampments. But subsequently, the magazine was hardly involved. According to Willie, *Adbusters* provided little material support for the occupation. "They provided a couple neat images, and the idea," he said, "but people on the ground in NYC did all the work."

When NYABC heard of the *Adbusters* call, the group "was extremely skeptical that something just put out on the Internet could [mobilize a protest of that size], but they decided to go along and see what happened," said Jackie. In Bloombergville, the central structure and decision-making process had been the General Assembly (GA), so NYABC decided to "call a General Assembly, see who showed up, and go from there."

On August 2, the first GA convened at the *Charging Bull* statue, A Wall Street icon located at the tip of Bowling Green Park. "Most people had had no experience with the GA," said Jackie. "So the meeting at the *Bull* was being run like a rally, with speakers. There even was a discussion to immediately, at the end of the speakers, march on Wall Street." Those who had showed up for a GA grew more and more impatient, until one activist, Georgia Sangri, finally shouted, "This is not a General Assembly," and persuaded a group of people to move to the other side of the *Bull* and talk in GA format. Many who attended that first, brief GA had heard of the *Adbusters* call, but they quickly dropped the idea of demanding a Presidential Commission. This first, brief GA concluded with a plan to reconvene, one week later, at the Irish Hunger Memorial in Battery Park, downtown Manhattan. The August 9 GA taught this new group how General Assemblies work–the nuts and bolts of the democratic process. From then on, the GA met each week in Tompkins Square Park, in Manhattan's Alphabet City.

The purpose of these August and early September GAs was to plan a major anti-Wall Street protest on September 17. In anticipation of this event, new committees formed: there was the Food Committee, which had raised $1,000 for supplies, the Student Committee, the Outreach Committee; the Internet Working Group; the Arts and Culture Working Group; and the Tactical Committee. Some organizers doubted that the protest would make an impact, but they still advocated for increased organization. As more and more people heard the *Adbusters* call, "even the people who had been skeptical at first felt like somebody's got to organize this, because people may show up!" Jackie said. Early GAs also recognized "it could be dangerous going to Wall Street, if people weren't prepared." So committees formed to address participants' fears. This preparation extended beyond safety concerns. Organizers worried that, if the event fizzled, all the momentum that had been building throughout the summer would fade. So the Outreach Committee charged itself with bringing people to GAs in order that meetings would continue, even if September 17 failed as an individual action. In addition, the Arts and Culture Working Group planned a New York Fun Exchange Carnival on Wall Street to coincide with September 17: they intended to use cultural activities to inspire political change.

Of the committees formed in the weeks leading up to September 17, the Tactical Committee, had perhaps the most impact. While the Outreach Committee worked to draw people to the GAs, and Arts and Culture sought to engage their imaginations, the Tactical Committee "determined the time and place for the first General Assembly to happen and everything that would need to be done in order for that to happen." They experimented with a few occupations to find out if it was possible to occupy a public park or Wall Street. At the beginning of September, some tried Tompkins Square Park, but the police immediately kicked them out when the park closed for the evening. Others, from Arts and Culture, tried to occupy Wall Street itself on September 1. The cops rounded them up and arrested them. One member of the committee revealed that the group was expecting "the police to be particularly repressive" on September 17. The plan was to "attempt to have a GA at one location" and then "move to a new place and then another place throughout the weekend." The group combed lower Manhattan for public parks and privately-owned public spaces that could hold at least 2,000 people. They wanted locations that were "close enough to Wall Street so that symbolism remained," and that also provided multiple exits, in case the police threatened to sweep the square for arrests.

Eight spaces fit the Tactical Committee's criteria–including Chase Manhattan Plaza, their first choice. When the Tactical Committee found out at noon on September 17 that "Chase Plaza was completely barricaded," and protesters "would be unable to hold a General Assembly there," members of the committee "went around to the other proposed locations–which were not released to anyone up until that point–and agreed that Zuccotti Park would be the best choice" to host that day's events. The organizers handed out copies of their previously undisclosed map of backup locations to "fellow trustworthy organizers" at 2:30 p.m. By 3:00 p.m., Occupy Wall Street was hosting its first official General Assembly and had found a new home in Zuccotti Park.

An Occupation is Born

*"People from past General Assemblies didn't come
[to Zuccotti Park] with sleeping bags—they
didn't expect to stay the night."*
—Marina Sitrin, member of OWS' Facilitators Working Group

Matt Presto, a teacher and graduate student who had participated in many of the planning meetings of the New York General Assembly in Tompkins Square Park, came home to his apartment on Friday night from a training where a small group of mostly young, mostly white men and women made last minute plans for Saturday, September 17. Anticipating possible arrest, he had emailed a co-worker, "Just so you know, I might not be at work on Monday." He stayed up late that night talking with six friends from Ohio who had come into New York for the Occupy Wall Street event. They discussed the likely behavior of the New York Police Department (NYPD): pepper spraying, kettling, baton beating, shoving people on the ground. They improvised first aid kits with bandages, gauze, and a solution of water and antacid for eyewash.

The NYPD was also preparing. Police Department chief spokesman Paul J. Browne told the *New York Times*, "No permits had been sought for the demonstration but plans for it were well known publicly." (Organizers suspected that their planning meetings had been infiltrated by police informants.) Saturday morning the city shut down sections of Wall Street near the New York Stock Exchange and Federal Hall. By 10:00 a.m. metal barricades manned by police officers ringed the blocks of Wall Street between Broadway and Williams Street.

Around noon Matt Presto arrived in Bowling Green Park, home to the famous statue of the Charging Bull. He found 400 or so people, "circling around the bull, chanting, signs and everything." At noon, a group sat down and leaned against the metal barricade blocking access to Wall Street, forming what OWS "First Communique" called a "spontaneous blockade." The police threatened to arrest the people sitting down, so they got up and marched away. By 2:00 p.m., nearly two dozen uniformed police officers surrounded the bull, while, as the *New York Times* delicately put it, "others worked to disperse the crowd." Meanwhile, various participants held impromptu yoga and tai chi classes in Bowling Green Park.

At 3 p.m. a crowd of about 1,000 began gathering, according to plan, at Chase Plaza. Reverend Billy Talen of the Church of Stop Shopping and Rosanne Barr gave addresses through a bullhorn. Trays of sliced bread and jars of Skippy peanut butter were passed around. Fruit was distributed from shopping carts.

The Tactical Committee had produced a map on which they had marked seven possible locations for a General Assembly to take place. At 2:30, several hundred photocopies of this map were handed out at Chase Plaza, along with the instruction to go to "Location Two"—Zuccotti Park—"in thirty minutes."

Bordered on the west by Trinity Place, on the east by Broadway, and with Liberty and Cedar Streets to its north and south, respectively, Zuccotti Park (widely known in the movement by its original, pre-2006 name of Liberty Square or Liberty Plaza) is nestled in the heart of Lower Manhattan—directly in between Wall Street and the former World Trade Center site.

The neighborhood is filled with tourists, as well as a mix of financial workers, retail service workers and hard-hatted laborers from the nearby Freedom Tower construction site. Although Zuccotti is privately-owned, the corporate owner has made the park public for zoning benefits and the location is no stranger to un-permitted political protest. (In the early summer of 2010, an anti-mosque rally was held there in which some 300 right-wing protesters defied a rejected permit request and filled the park's western side with anti-Muslim signs as well as American and Gadsden flags for the better part of an afternoon.)

The crowd marched across the financial district chanting "Wall Street is our street" and "Power to the people not to the banks." At Zuccotti Park a food committee passed out sandwiches and water while people sang, danced, and watched puppets.

Although a General Assembly had been announced for 3:00 p.m., "It was decided we would go into small breakout groups to have discussions about what people wanted to see come out of this and why they were interested in Occupy Wall Street," Matt Presto recalled. "We spent a lot of time trying to explain the process, because this was new for a lot of people."

According to Marina Sitrin, a member of OWS's Facilitators Working Group, who teaches at the City University of New York, the original idea was to have "political discussion about why you are frustrated" with the state of the world and "what inspires you, what would you like to see in the world?" Talk soon turned to plans for the occupation itself. "What people came to Zuccotti Park prepared to talk about, was how they were going to occupy, what it was going to look like, and what tomorrow looks like." Participants "wanted to get down to the question: So, are we going to occupy, or are we not going to occupy?"

Many of those who had participated in the previous New York General Assembly meetings in Tompkins Square Park were doubtful that OWS had a future. Marina noted that "People from past General Assemblies didn't come with sleeping bags—they didn't expect to stay the night." Her fellow facilitator, Marisa Holmes, recalls, "I along with many others, expected that it would fizzle out in a couple of days."

As the time for the General Assembly approached, a group of 40 or 50 gathered to figure out how to run it. Finally, Marina, Marisa, and a few others who had been in the Tompkins Square General Assemblies agreed to facilitate it. Marina recalls,

> It was beautiful and powerful. We started with megaphones, and it didn't work very well. We were standing in the center up on one of the benches and everyone was standing around in a mass circle, so we had to speak in two directions. After ten or fifteen minutes we put the megaphones down and I spoke to the people in front of me using the people's mic, which is something that we had practiced in facilitator training two nights previously. I had participated in it and seen it used in Seattle in the 1999 WTO protests, but I had thought of it as something useful on the street for communicating information. I actually hadn't thought of it as a way of conducting an assembly. But we were standing in the center of a group of two thousand people and megaphones were not working.

She spoke a few words to the people closest by, then asked them to repeat it in unison to the others.

> "That first night using the people's mic, people hadn't done it before, but immediately picked up on it. It creates an atmosphere of active listening and participation. As soon as we started the people's mic, the vibe and energy totally changed."

The General Assembly decided that the group would occupy Zuccotti Park overnight and hold a General Assembly at 10:00 a.m. the next morning. About 300 people settled down in sleeping bags for the night while the police waited nearby.

Matt Presto remembers "feeling pleasantly surprised" but "still on edge about what would happen next," and thinking, "How long could the police tolerate this? They'll probably break us up Sunday evening or Monday."

* * *

Alexandre de Carvalho, a 28-year-old from Rio de Janiero who had been part of the Arts and Culture committee since the planning of the occupation, described his first night in the park. "It was cold and it hurt," he said. Tents weren't allowed, and most occupiers had only thin sleeping bags and cardboard boxes between them and the pavement.

Alex woke up around six in the morning, after only two hours of real sleep, uncertain of what the first full day of occupation would become. "We still hadn't figured out what to do," he said.

Amy Roberts, now a co-founder of the OWS archive, picked up on that uncertainty when she visited the occupation in its first days. "I wasn't sure what to make of it. It was just completely different from anything I'd seen before," she said, confessing she thought the occupiers "naïve" at first. "I had been active in so many things for so many years without seeing them go anywhere that I wasn't sure if I wanted to get involved. But I kept coming back." Early discussions among the occupiers were, she says, mainly concerned with "how to relate to the police, and then how to just organize the discussions."

On the first full day of occupation, police asked occupiers to remove signs taped to park trees Sunday morning, and the question of whether or not to obey absorbed the 10 a.m. General Assembly. At around noon a group, tired of talk, broke off from the GA and began to march around the square, chanting and urging others to join. Soon a large crowd danced down Broadway towards Battery Park in the September sun, beckoning to tourists and chanting, "It's more fun than shopping!"

The facilitators were good-natured about being interrupted; when the marchers returned they met them with applause and announced that the General Assembly would reconvene at 3 p.m. But the episode raised doubts about whether or not the group's energy could be channeled effectively into the consensus process.

These doubts were put to rest when the assembly reconvened at 3 p.m. This time, the assembly did not disperse until 10:30 p.m. and it managed to reach some important decisions about how occupiers would relate to the police and to each other: There would be no official police liaison; the tactics working group would be empowered to scout out alternative locations if they were forced from Zuccotti.

Even as the occupation was figuring out how to define itself, it was already inspiring support from people around the country and the world. Justin Wedes, a member of the Food working group, explained that after 24 hours, occupiers had grown tired of fruit and PB&J. His group cast about online for local Mom and Pop joints that could deliver warm food and were pleased to find one with a name that seemed "really in line with our mission": Liberato's Pizza. Wedes tweeted out calls for pizza orders and within hours the restaurant was "inundated with calls from around the world" by people ordering food for the protesters on their credit cards. Occupiers had to send a group to help pick up pizzas–the staff wasn't large enough to keep up with the world's desire to feed the burgeoning movement.

On Tuesday morning, it began to rain and occupiers moved to protect their belongings and media equipment with suspended tarps. According to the Web site occupywallst.org one of the main online forums of the movement, police moved in with bull horns at around 7 a.m., declaring the tarps illegal. Occupiers held an emergency General Assembly and decided to hold the tarps up themselves.

According to the NYPD, however, human-held tarps were

still structures. Police began to rip tarps away from the occupiers. When one young man sat down on a tarp protecting media equipment, police threw him to the ground, face first, and then arrested him. Another video posted on the site showed police dragging a protester from the park to the sidewalk by his feet and denying an asthmatic arrestee an inhaler. In total, seven were arrested that day and the police walked off with arms full of confiscated blue tarps.

By Wednesday, despite the best efforts of the weather and the NYPD, Zuccotti Park had become a sort of makeshift village that would capture the popular imagination for the next three months. Information desks at the park's entrances announced a daily schedule: daily marches on Wall Street timed with the opening and closing bells, general assemblies at 1 p.m. and 7 p.m. There were medics on duty. The kitchen crew had set up their own workstation. Colorful cardboard signs decorated the pavement. And the drumming circle kept on drumming, rain or shine.

It was Wednesday's General Assembly, Amy Roberts said, that convinced her to stick around. On Monday night, the assembly had broken up into small groups to draft Principles of Solidarity. Those principles had been combined and consolidated by a working group, and now the assembly was breaking into groups once again to further discuss and edit the draft. Listening to the brainstorm, Roberts said, "I was very impressed with how—just the idealism of everyone, you know, the optimism."

The same working group then gathered everyone's comments and edits into a second draft of Principles of Solidarity, presented to the General Assembly on Friday, September 23. After four blocks were presented and worked through, the GA moved again for consensus. The anonymous taker of the GA minutes that day recorded that "everyone was thrilled that consensus had been reached and the document would be posted online, in one of the most beautiful examples of a true democracy that I, personally, have ever seen."

The Principles of Solidarity, the first official document produced by the occupation, were and are:

- Engaging in direct and transparent participatory democracy;
- Exercising personal and collective responsibility;
- Recognizing individuals' inherent privilege and the influence it has on all interactions;
- Empowering one another against all forms of oppression;
- Redefining how labor is valued;
- The sanctity of individual privacy;
- The belief that education is a human right; and
- Endeavoring to practice and support wide application of open source.

In addition to working out its defining principles that week, OWS was also starting to build solidarity with other causes and organizations. On the morning of Thursday, September 22, OWS activists disrupted a Sotheby's art auction in support of locked-out art handlers unionized by Teamsters Local 814. Then, at around 7 p.m. the same night, a Union Square protest against Georgia death row prisoner Troy Davis's execution started an impromptu march down to Zuccotti Park. Together, the marchers and the occupiers headed over to Wall Street. The popular, "Whose street? Our street!" changed to, "Whose street? Troy's street!" as protesters showed the country's financial capital that it would now join federal, state, and municipal buildings as a default receptor of public rage.

On Saturday, September 24, after a week of daily marches to Wall Street for the opening and closing bell, activists decided to march uptown. One of the marchers, Brennan Cavanaugh, was surprised and excited to find the crowd heading up Broadway, against traffic. "At that point I was like, this is the kind of march

I can get behind—an unpermitted guerilla march. And people were just shouting, 'All Day, All Week: Occupy Wall Street!' The police didn't know what to do, it seemed. They kept trying to block the streets from the people marching north but the people would just go around them."

According to Cavanaugh, the march began to lose steam when it reached Union Square, and demonstrators were unsure of where to move next. That was when the police moved in, blocking 12th Street, University Place and Fifth Avenue with orange netting. The movement had appeared quiet, but the dynamic changed when Deputy Inspector Anthony Bologna pepper sprayed a group of mostly women who were already contained within orange police netting. The video of the incident, in which a young woman suddenly drops to her knees with a scream and buries her face in her arms, immediately went viral on the Internet and was widely broadcast by mainstream media. Cavanaugh called it the "scream heard round the world." The OWS message had been gaining traction all through the previous week. But the images of police violence on September 24 seemed to give the movement further momentum.

A total of 80 activists were arrested that day, including Cavanaugh. "I was photographing someone who had their face shoved to the ground and was being arrested and they rolled out the orange netting behind me. I heard the slap of plastic on the ground. And I went to step over it and as soon as I stepped over it, they lifted it up and I got caught in between it. A guy who I had never seen before, a plain-clothed man, came around and grabbed my wrist and put a zip tie on me."

Cavanaugh sat in a cell with other protesters for three hours. He was released at 3 a.m. more fully committed to the movement than ever. "After that," he says, "I was down with this whole thing."

The General Assembly

*"If people aren't being respectful of others' identities,
or are speaking from a limited perspective, that will be added
into the conversation. People will be called out on it".*
—*DiceyTroop, General Assembly Twitter reporter*

The General Assembly, an extraordinary nightly display of consensual democracy in action, soon became one of the defining experiences of Occupy Wall Street. No one attending its meetings, generally held at 7 p.m. each evening in the shadow of the big red statue at the east end of Zuccotti, could fail to be impressed, indeed often moved, by the spirit of community engendered by the GA, as it came to be known.

Participants, on some evenings numbering in the thousands, sat on the steps running down from Broadway, or huddled together at their foot, on the paving of the park. Behind them, activists gathered in serried rows, some on the low walls of the flower planters, others stretching off into the copse of small trees that forms a parasol over the interior of the park. The meeting was addressed from the steps, with speakers distinguished only by the fact they were on their feet, surrounded by the GA's facilitators, bellowing their words in the steady, rhythmic cadence that the "people's mic" demands.

The diversity of the crowd was immediately apparent. Those sleeping in the park, with the grimy demeanor and clothing that signaled the rigors of camping out, stood next to smartly attired office workers, who had apparently dropped by on a detour from their evening commute; older activists, dressed as if they had just returned from hearing Country Joe play Woodstock, sat crammed next to college students who dressed, well, pretty much the same way.

What unified this disparate throng was a tangible sense of solidarity, a commitment to the cause of the occupation, but also an evident commitment to each other. It was not unusual for food, packets of biscuits or pretzels, or bottles of water to be passed hand-to-hand around the rows, shared by strangers who had just become comrades. The crowd was united also by a gentle but firm resolve to respect the rights of others, to space, to be heard, to be whoever they were.

This respectfulness extended to the facilitators running the meetings, whose patience and good nature in the face of often arcane and protracted procedural negotiations bordered on the superhuman. Identifying themselves only by their first names, and rotating responsibility, both within each meeting and on different nights, their effort not to appear in any way as "leaders" seemed admirable, if sometimes less than convincing. Running a meeting of hundreds or thousands, without amplification and under rules which many present found unfamiliar, required considerable charisma and eloquence, qualities that the young people facilitating the GA evidenced in spades.

Those who spoke at the GA often did so with barely suppressed emotion. Hearing one's words echoing off the bankers' towers surrounding the park as they were repeated, sometimes up to three times, by expanding concentric circles of the crowd, was evidently an experience both strange and profoundly moving. At the GA on the night following the eviction of the tents from the park, more than one speaker openly expressed love for the assembly, a declaration that would have surely seemed saccharine and disingenuous in more conventional gatherings, but here was received, without embarrassment, as an authentic act of communion.

Formally, the GA served a prosaic function: it was the decision-making body of the action and the forum through which organizers made sure that the needs of those participating were met—reports from groups dealing with food, legal and medical assistance, sanitation, and security took up much of the agenda. But the GA also provided a place for protesters to air grievances, decide on direct actions, and debate movement strategy, among other things. Although its use of the people's mic and consensual decision-making often proved frustratingly clumsy and time-consuming for resolving detailed issues, as a means of bonding and establishing the broad principles of the action, the GA proved highly effective.

The facilitation working group took responsibility for preparing the agendas, calling the meeting to order, and quieting a sometimes distracted crowd. The facilitators were trained prior to hosting their first GA and so were familiar with the techniques that enabled them to let all opinions be heard in the most respectful and efficient way. In order to prevent the emergence of an entrenched leadership, facilitators were not allowed to lead two meetings in a row and so rotated dates and responsibilities. New facilitators were paired with those who were more experienced so that a basic skill level was maintained throughout.

To the uninitiated, the GA could sometimes seem overwhelming, unfocused and unproductive. Even some of those who had participated in previous actions, and were thus familiar with the precepts of participation, consensus, and transparency that underpinned the running of the GA, were surprised to see the model attempted in a public space with such large numbers present. To help address the problems this inhered, facilitators took the first few minutes of each meeting to explain the mechanisms through which the GA operated.

First were the hand signals that made it possible for the crowd to communicate *en masse* with each other and with the facilitators. The most frequently used of these gestures is called *twinkling*. A wiggling of the fingers with either one or both hands raised, twinkling originated as a symbol in American Sign Language to express applause. Over the course of OWS, its use evolved and expanded as Marina Sitrin, whose experience as a facilitator stretches back to the 1999 Seattle anti-WTO mobilizations, explained, ". . . by twinkling you see the reaction of the person next to you. Are they happy or not? Are they liking it? The language has started to change so now when people talk about twinkling, it's not silent applause, it's *do ya like it?* Now there's the temperature check, so there's twinkling in the middle and twinkling down below. Twinkling with your fingers straight in front of you means I'm on the fence. This is the language people use, *I'm in the middle.* And then wiggling your fingers in a downward direction is *I'm not liking it, I'm not feeling it.* The first time I've ever seen it [the temperature check] is in Occupy Wall Street and I've been in a lot of big democratic spaces. I like it because it's a way of shouting out, without the shouting."

A range of other hand gestures is commonly used at GAs: *Point of process* is signaled by forming a triangle with the thumbs and index fingers. It indicates that a transgression of the agreed procedures of the meeting has occurred, perhaps by someone speaking out of turn or off-topic, and constitutes a request that the facilitators move the discussion back on track. *Point of information* involves raising one hand with an extended index finger and is used to convey that the signaler has an important fact related to the matter under consideration. *Clarification* is made by curling one hand into a C shape, and indicates that a person is confused and needs to ask a question to better understand the discussion. And the *wrap it up* signal is made by a rolling motion of the hands and is meant to convey, in a loving and respectful way of course, as the facilitators always stress, that the person speaking should draw their comments to a close and step back so others have a chance to talk.

Of all the signals used in the GA, the *block* is the most consequential. It is expressed by the crossing of arms over one's chest and it indicates a serious moral or practical objection to the proposal. Facilitators regularly caution against overuse of the signal, explaining that it is an extreme measure, indicating that the objector will leave the group if her or his concerns are not addressed. Typically, the person making the block will explain the reasoning behind their objection and offer a "friendly amendment," designed to make the proposal under discussion something that can be supported.

Like many other aspects of OWS procedures, the use of hand signals has a long history. According to Marina, ". . . the tools and language [that OWS uses] originate with the Quakers. We're talking about generations, the anti-war movement, the feminist movement; a lot of different social movements in the U.S. have used different forms of consensus that include [facilitation] tools." Marina also pointed out that, because they are silent, the hand gestures were particularly useful in large assemblies where clapping or cheering would use up time that could be otherwise devoted to the business of the meeting, a consideration of particular importance for proceedings being conducted at the tortoise tempo of the people's mic.

The other major structural component of the GA is the use of the *progressive stack* to order crowd comments on proposals. During the early days of the GA, when it was being held in Tompkins Square, the core organizing group realized that, despite their openness and desire for diversity, the majority of those taking the floor remained stubbornly white and male. As a response to this inequity, a decision was made to give preference to those groups such as women and people of color whose voices are typically less often heard. Orchestrating *progressive stack* is part of the role of the *stack-taker* who recognizes those wishing to speak to the GA. "If people aren't being respectful of others' identities, or are speaking from a limited perspective, that will be added into the conversation. People will be called out on it. The process makes it easier to do that," explains DiceyTroop, a member of the press team who has live-tweeted GA meetings.

This sensitivity to inequities that exist in society at large is part of a fundamental unease on the part of OWS organizers towards any form of hierarchical structure. Another feature of the introductory segment of the GA is an explanation of the idea of *step-up/step-back*. This concept encourages those requesting time to speak to consider whether they might "step up" by recognizing their relatively privileged role in society at large and cede the floor, or "step back," to allow someone from a group with traditionally less opportunities to have their voice heard.

The hand signals, progressive stack and step-up/step-back are key components of how GA facilitators try ensure genuine democracy at the meetings. Having explained their use at the outset of proceedings they then introduce the agenda for the meeting. On most evenings this is a mix of proposals, working group report backs, and announcements. During this section of the meeting, those in the crowd are discouraged from any lengthy exposition of their opinions and business moves at as brisk a pace as the people's mic, points of information, requests for clarification, amendments, and temperature checks allow. The chance for those present to speak off the cuff comes towards the end of the GA with a session called, appropriately enough, the soapbox. This period of the meeting, perhaps unsurprisingly, can stretch for long hours into the night, with often a dwindling audience, but the same rules of affirmative speaking and respect for the rights of others to be heard apply.

Over time the procedures of the GA have become more

sophisticated. Latterly, for example, working groups bringing proposals to the GA are required to post them on the OWS Web site 48 hours ahead of time so that people can prepare their responses and plan their attendance to coincide with items they consider of particular importance. Furthermore, the GA is now no longer the only decision-making body within OWS: The formation of a Spokes Council, consisting of representatives from each of the working groups, was latterly agreed on so that the movement could more easily coordinate financial and legal decision making.

The GA does not always function smoothly. Its proceedings can easily be derailed by people making unnecessary calls for a mic check or superfluous points of information. Though the use of the block is generally restrained, it can on occasion throw otherwise broad consensus into chaos. Moreover, the fact that the meetings are held publicly, open to anyone who cares to show up, and with the intention of giving voice to everyone present who wishes to speak, poses a number of problems. The meetings can be populated by people entirely unfamiliar with OWS proceedings or, worse, unsympathetic to its aims. The crowd varies in both size and character from one meeting to the next, most of those present are not attending consecutive meetings and for some this will be their first and only visit. Especially since the eviction, the issue of who is participating in the GA has become particularly acute. Anyone carrying a large bag, a group that includes many of the original occupiers who stayed overnight as well as some of the homeless, has been denied entry to the park by the police and thus prevented from attending the meetings.

In the face of difficulties intrinsic to the GA process, facilitators and organizers have continued their work to make the meetings more accessible. Emergency proposals can be taken at the GA even though they have not been circulated in advance, minutes of proceedings are posted to the OWS Web site, and a live account of what's happening is conveyed in real time by the press team using social media. DiceyTroop is just one of those who have taken responsibility for live-tweeting the GAs and Spokes Councils. Live streaming via video blogs such as The Other 99% also helps to get the word out.

Debates about how to refine and develop the process continue apace and important questions remain as to whether the General Assembly model can maintain a genuinely democratic movement as it develops beyond the first flush of enthusiasm of a new movement. But for those lucky enough to have been present in Zuccotti during those heady evenings of early fall 2011, the OWS General Assembly has provided a trove of inspiring and unforgettable memories, and a pointer to a new way of doing politics.

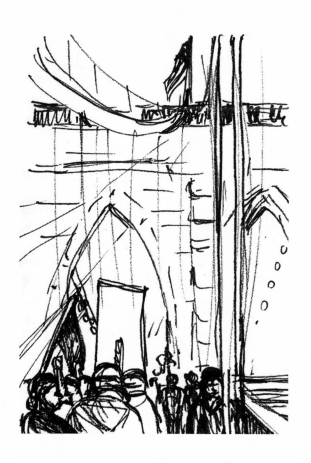

Brooklyn Bridge

"I want you guys to know . . . I totally know where you're coming from. My family was fucked over by foreclosures and predatory loans and the banking industry being twisted . . . but I can't be with you guys because of this badge"
—*Police officer arresting protesters on the Brooklyn Bridge*

On October 1, 2011, more than 1,000 gathered at Zuccotti Park to protest the incident, one week prior, in which NYPD deputy inspector Anthony Bologna pepper sprayed three young female protesters in the face while they were corralled behind orange mesh fencing during a march near Union Square. The attack was captured on video and made the rounds on YouTube, prompting outrage among New Yorkers and galvanizing OWS supporters across the country. In response, a march was planned to target one of New York City's most iconic landmarks—the Brooklyn Bridge.

Around 3 p.m. that Saturday, behind a banner reading "We The People," the march stepped off from Zuccotti, heading north on Broadway. Stretching for blocks, marchers carried signs reading, "Let's Get Free," "The Future Isn't What It Used To Be," "Corruption & Greed Are NOT American" and "You Are Loved," and chanted slogans like, "How do we end this deficit? Stop the war! Tax the rich!" and its sardonic counterpart, "Start the war! Eat the rich!" After about a half hour, the marchers began to approach the bridge, where confusion quickly set in. The march fractured, creating a bottle-neck at the bridge's entrance, with some choosing the pre-approved pedestrian walkway, and others boldly striking out for the bridge's motorway entrance. Those who chose the roadway quickly came upon a handful of police, mostly senior officers in their white shirts with a megaphone and only a few zip-ties between them, standing in the march's path. One of the officers attempted to issue a warning over his megaphone, but chants of "Take the bridge! Take the bridge!" drowned him out. Sensing an opportunity, those on the march's front line soon locked arms and, assured by the mass of people chanting behind them, began a slow, purposeful advance on the police and onto the bridge's roadway. Severely outnumbered, the handful of police on the bridge turned and walked toward Brooklyn, all the while shouting on their radios. As the march took the roadway, several protesters who had taken the pedestrian walk hopped the railing to join the occupation of the bridge.

But as marchers swarmed the roadway chanting, "We are the 99 percent!" "Banks got bailed out! We got sold out!" and "Whose bridge? Our bridge!" the police quickly regrouped and established a barricade using the increasingly ubiquitous orange mesh fence, which was unfurled mid-span to stop them. Those near the front of the march, halted in their tracks, could not see the back of the march from the bridge's center, but whispers began to circulate that the police had completely enclosed them. Although the protesters who remained on the pedestrian walkway were allowed to continue moving, those who had spilled onto the roadway below were kettled in the net. The orange netting, which in the preceding weeks had become synonymous with arrest, surprised many protesters, who figured that their peaceful protest was not violating the law and who had not heard police warnings not to enter the roadway. "One of the things that you always know is that if the cops don't want you to go somewhere, you don't. They block it. It doesn't happen," said a People's Librarian who was arrested on the bridge but wished to remain anonymous. "So for all intents and purposes, it looked like the cops were just leading the march on the bridge. That's where we went and that's when they kettled us."

Others like Mandy, a People's Librarian who had traveled with her husband from their home in Indiana to attend the march, figured those on the roadway were volunteering for arrest. "They're not going to let us shut down the Brooklyn Bridge. Everyone on the bridge is going to jail," Mandy recalled thinking. "We assumed that everybody on the bridge knew they were going to jail; we were surprised later to find out that some people didn't know that." Initially, Mandy and her husband had walked onto the roadway—but when they saw the police beginning to kettle they thought of their two young children and made quick use of their Midwestern charm. "We just walked to the police line looking all upper-middle-classy, white and said, 'Oh dear, we need to get through, officers.'" The ploy worked and the two were allowed off the bridge. Amy Roberts, a cofounder of the OWS archive working group, also found a way past the orange net. "They let a few women go," she said. Amy said a man who claimed to be with the American Civil Liberties Union asked her and a few others whether they had been asked to disperse. When they replied that they had been given no such order, the man spoke to the police, who let them go. "It was clear to me that he wasn't from the ACLU, but I was glad to be let go," Amy said. "I was worried about losing my job. And I was like, I don't know if I want to lose my job just for this. It was all these things that were going through my head."

For those 700-or-so marchers who could not pass as tourists or who otherwise did not manage to escape the orange net, they soon found themselves trapped on the Brooklyn Bridge, facing certain arrest. Some, especially near the front line, attempted to resist, but were quickly pressed to the asphalt by officers. "One by one the police snatch the protesters, and it dawns on everyone that they have enough zip-tie cuffs for all of us," recalled one marcher who was arrested that afternoon. "That they probably have one for each person in the city." As the mass-arrest began, protesters were lined up on either side of the street facing the middle. Those tied let out cheers and whistles for the new arrestees, many of whom in turn smiled and strutted as though they were on a catwalk. Spirits remained high among many, who recognized that in being arrested they were halting bridge traffic—they were occupying the bridge even as they were arrested for doing so. Soon large prison buses and police wagons pulled up to collect the hundreds who stood cuffed and waiting.

One of those waiting to be taken to police processing shortly after 4 p.m. was Keith, a 24-year-old U.S. Navy veteran who had been carrying a sign reading "Fire Your Boss!" While Keith had never considered himself an activist, he said he had been paying more attention to current events of late and felt drawn to OWS because he was fed up with the influence of money and the banks on politics. "If there's one thing that the military should and does teach an individual it's to step up and sort of take charge and responsibility and accountability of your actions and to be a leader," Keith said. While Keith had originally taken the pedestrian walkway, looking down on those in the roadway inspired him and he could not stand to be contained. "I urged the people I was walking with to hop the railing and get on the road and take the bridge," Keith recalled. "At the time we didn't think about how the bridge was being taken. So we just went and until we were stopped, and then essentially kettled, and then everybody was detained." He described his arrest as both "casual" and confusing. "I was very compliant, I didn't resist," Keith said. "But when the officer put the cuffs on me, I turned around and started talking to him." The officer was unmoved by Keith's veteran status, and he was loaded into a police wagon with nine others. As his van drove off hundreds of others remained handcuffed on the bridge, and others chanted "Shame! Shame! Shame!" and "You belong with us! We're fighting for your pensions!" at the police from the pedestrian walkway.

Of the prisoner transport wagon, one arrestee recalled, "As soon as the officers shut the heavy metal doors, it gets incredibly hot." The sweat induced by the heat enabled some of the 10 or 12 arrestees in one wagon to slip out of their plastic ties (later slipped back on before the officers could protest) and pour bottled water into the mouths of those who remained cuffed. That van was driven around for about an hour, before parking—the arrestees were then forced to sit in the tight, hot space for hours awaiting processing. They took turns sitting on the cooler floor and did their best to conserve water. "But it isn't all bad," recalled the same anonymous arrestee, "A college student named Amanda pulls out her phone and plays the classic Against Me! sing-along, 'Baby I'm An Anarchist.'" Discussions in the wagons also turned to socializing and some small talk about tactics and the future of OWS. Some of the connections made in prisoner vans and holding cells would stick once protesters returned to Zuccotti. "That was one of the things that had kind of always been my problem when I was coming down before [the arrest] . . . I'd always be like, hanging around, doing odds and ends but I didn't feel like I really knew people," recalled one People's Librarian who was arrested on the bridge. "But now, after that point, it was like 'Hey!' 'You been keeping out of trouble!?' 'Keep your nose clean!'"

Once arrested marchers were released from vans and buses, they were photographed and their bags and possessions confiscated. Recalled one arrestee, "Processing is a slow shuffle from space to space, and the station is packed. We're drenched with sweat and enjoying the relatively open air." A hand-written sign hanging in the jail told officers to write "4:20 p.m." as the time of arrest for all of the 700-plus protesters. They were charged with disorderly conduct and violating roadway laws through obstruction—a charge that irked many, seeing as the marchers were moving in the direction of traffic and it was the police who stopped and then contained them, thus causing the obstruction. "To me that feels like entrapment," Keith, the Navy vet, said.

Keith's group was the first to be dropped off for processing at One Police Plaza, a short drive from the Bridge. While waiting to be emptied out of the wagon back at the precinct, a police officer came into the truck. "He looked each of us in the eye," Keith reported, "and he said, 'Listen to me, your protest is over. Your day is over. You have made your point. We hear you.'" The officer then paused, and added something Keith said he never expected to hear. "I want you guys to know," the officer continued, "I'm right there with you. I totally know where you're coming from. My family was fucked over by foreclosures and predatory loans and the banking industry being twisted. I'm with you guys but I can't be with you guys because of this badge. But you should know I feel the same way." Leading them off the wagon, he then added, "So cut the shit, be compliant, and do what you need to do to get out of here as soon as you can and go home."

As more groups of the arrested protesters began arriving at the police precincts, cries of solidarity and cheers went up as new people were loaded into the holding cells. Those arrested included students, a structural architect in his mid-20s, a jocular finance student from Ontario visiting New York for the first time. By one count, there were 117 men in one of the holding cells over the course of three hours, and another 40 or 50 women in another cell. But despite the crowding, according to several of the arrested protesters the mood in the cells was, at times, buoyant. "Throughout the night it was weird, because you think that people would be really sad, but for the 117 of us in that cell, it was the best situation any of us could be in because we had solidarity. What possible response do you think you could get from these people other than us wanting to go back and activate ourselves even more? If you arrest one of us, two more will show up." Other cells were smaller—8' x 10' with a non-functional sink, a bench with a pad and a plain toilet bowl. The food offered to protesters as they awaited processing included peanut butter or cheese sandwiches and a carton of milk apiece. "From a cell over we hear laughing suggestions that we should reject the 1 percent milk in solidarity with the 99 percent," recalled one arrestee.

Like many of his fellow detainees, Keith was eventually released at 3:30 a.m. on October 2—nearly 12 hours after his arrest. He said he then went home and went to sleep. But first thing the next morning Keith headed right back down to Zuccotti. "I went to the information center and said, 'What can I do?'"

60 Wall Street

"I'm one of the people still sleeping out at the park . . . last night we had thirty of us, and only two umbrellas. If you are going straight home after this, consider stopping by the park to donate your umbrella so we can stay dry out there tonight."
—*Visitor to an OWS book group meeting at 60 Wall Street*

If Zuccotti Park was, as of September 17, the primary address of the Occupy Wall Street movement, then surely the movement's second home was the atrium of a skyscraper at 60 Wall Street. The atrium, technically a privately-owned public space with set rules restricting its use, like Zuccotti Park, the atrium is massive, brightly lit, and visually striking: latticed, mirrored columns sprout along its length from a hard black-and-white marble floor with benches of dark gray; granite-like stone wraps around their bases; both ends of the space feature entrances walled in glass; a third, internal wall is lined by similarly glassed-in cafés; and, incongruously, this would-be sanctuary in one of the most urban cities on earth boasts artificial waterfalls and palm trees. For Wall Street businessmen, the space functioned as a retreat, a place where they could eat their lunch away from the madness of the trading floor, while for some at the other extreme of America's socioeconomic ladder—the homeless—it was a spot to sit and perhaps play chess, limited only by the opening hours of 7 a.m.–10 p.m.

Since shortly after September 17, the atrium has also served as a place where Occupy Wall Street supporters can rest and mingle and, perhaps more significantly, has become the designated meeting place for a number of the movement's more visible and important working groups. The space took time to develop into this role. Speaking of her own Arts and Culture working group, Imani J. Brown recalled, "When I first got to 60 Wall Street, very few people were meeting there." But just slightly over a month later, Ms. Brown added, hundreds used it "all day, every day." Afternoons and evenings feature a succession of well-attended working group meetings: in addition to the Arts and Culture group, between 2 p.m. and roughly 8 p.m. the Direct Action working group meets, along with the Facilitation working group, which is charged with helping function smoothly the Structure working group, Environmentalist Solidarity; OWS en Español—Spanish-language liaisons for the movement—and, possibly most important of all, the Finance working group. Entering the atrium from either Wall Street to the south or Pine Street to the north, the sound that hits one's ears is particular: the low, constant hum of human voices, a steady buzz, punctuated by the odd exclamation. It is the sound of concerted, excited, cooperative activity.

The feel of being at 60 Wall Street reflects this dynamism. To walk into the atrium through the revolving doors at either end of the space means passing by the steady trickle, if not outright stream, of people flowing in and out throughout the day. It means walking past a security detail that, since OWS began using the atrium, features uniformed NYPD officers in addition to the space's own personnel. These are powerfully built men dressed in combat boots and what are unmistakably dark blue BDUs—Battle Dress Uniforms, military fatigues that come complete with matching army-style caps. As they pace the length of the atrium, or merely stand, mutely flanking the entrances, they are a visible, constant reminder that at 60 Wall Street, just as at Liberty Plaza, things are not exactly business as usual.

Inside the atrium, meanwhile, people, groups, and events are in constant motion. The only structure to the meetings that take place between the space's massive columns is that which the working groups themselves have imposed: setting up an area in which to meet is as simple (and yet, given the traffic flowing through, also as complicated) as commandeering one of the many round sheet-metal lawn tables furnishing the atrium, or finding enough chairs to make a circle. Over the course of a day, and despite official signs asking guests to replace chairs they move, this process of claiming and reclaiming furniture leaves the atrium in disarray, chairs scattered randomly around and at some distance from tables. There is no official signage for group meetings. The sign for a meeting of the Finance working group might be written large on a sheet of cardboard or it might not; a sign could be nothing more than a stray word scrawled on an errant piece of notebook paper, or a meeting might not have a sign at all.

Meetings too have a certain fluidity and unpredictability. Perhaps most memorably, periodic announcements of planned fire drills and equipment tests blast jarringly from loudspeakers far above with great frequency but, somehow, always at a moment when occupiers least expect it. Upon one of these announcements every meeting then in progress will grind to a halt, often mid-discussion, forcing occupiers to hold their thoughts until, as much as a minute or two later, the offending announcement has quieted. Yet Occupy Wall Street is nothing if not adaptable, used to interruptions from authorities: typically, a pause follows, speakers gather themselves, and then the low hum of occupation business being done resumes.

Attendance at working group meetings proves similarly unpredictable and fluid. As working groups carry on discussion around tables and encircled chairs, other occupiers constantly mill about, floating from working group to working group individually or in small clusters. Sometimes these wanderers are lost: "Is this Media?" one might ask. "Is this Comfort?" or, "Is this Poetry?" Signs do not help—even when a group has one, it is either ambiguous or simply goes unread. "Can you tell me where Comfort is meeting?" the visitor might continue. Often though, the visitor is not lost. but comes to make an announcement, usually related in some way to General Assembly business: "Sorry to interrupt," one such visitor declared, "but the weather out there is pretty bad, so the GA is going to set up here in about fifteen minutes." Another came with a plea: "I'm one of the people still sleeping out at the park . . . last night we had 30 of us, and only two umbrellas. If you are going straight home after this, consider stopping by the park to donate your umbrella so we can stay dry out there tonight." Most commonly, though, these roving participants come neither lost nor armed with an agenda of their own, but are rather engaged in a form of meandering, informal, simultaneous participation in the proceedings of many working groups. Such a newcomer might stand just outside a group's circle of chairs, lean against a column at a meeting's outer edges, or pace around the gathering, the better to hear the many different opinions being voiced. They actively participate, nodding their approval or disapproval of particular ideas and, once they feel they have listened long enough to grasp a group's topic of discussion, they frequently chime in with their own reactions and suggestions. True to the ethos of transparency and openness that lies at the heart of the Occupy movement, these new, casual, and usually temporary additions to the working groups are generally received with open arms and in the spirit of cooperation. Indeed, this ambulatory pool of added insight represents not just one of the idiosyncrasies that makes the experience of being at 60 Wall Street unique, but also a welcome source of intellectual capital for the working groups that meet there.

Though unique, the experience of meeting at 60 Wall Street is not strange to anyone who has attended a General Assembly, or, for that matter, who has even a passing familiarity with the trappings of the consensus-oriented decision-making process that underpins virtually all Occupy Wall Street business. Working group meetings feature facilitators just as the General Assembly does, and here, as in Zuccotti Park, their responsibility is to ensure that meetings progress smoothly and that all participants have the opportunity to make their voices heard. Meeting agendas and "stacks" impose order on meeting business and discussion. And the by now well-known devices for signaling consensus often seen at Zuccotti Park, such as the "twinkling" of fingers up, down, or horizontally to indicate approval, disapproval, or ambivalence, are just as evident here, especially given the at times significant decisions made by working groups in this space. Occupy Wall Street's Structure working group, which produced the highly contentious innovation that was the Spokes Council, holds its meetings in the atrium every day at 6 p.m.

The importance to Occupy Wall Street of these working group meetings and of the space in which they take place cannot be overstated, especially in the wake of the movement's partial eviction from Zuccotti Park on November 15. All at once, 60 Wall Street became the headquarters of the movement's organizational counteroffensive: as the dust from the NYPD raid settled, the newly-formed Housing working group, charged with the arduous task of finding housing for occupiers who can now no longer camp at Zuccotti Park, began meeting twice daily in the space. As winter approaches, 60 Wall Street has also become a space where groups that do not otherwise meet there, including the General Assembly, can gather, sheltered, when inclement weather threatens.

But in the end, the atrium is not merely a place for official business. As the fall wore on, and cold weather crept into New York, ordinary occupiers also turned to the atrium as a warm place to gather, most especially after the movement's November eviction removed any possibility of finding the shelter of a tent, sleeping bag, or even a simple tarp at Zuccotti Park. Nor did 60 Wall Street entirely lose its previous character when OWS moved in. Businessmen can still frequently be seen eating in, or passing through, the space, and the homeless—and yes, their chess games—similarly remain a constant presence. Appropriately enough, the result is a space and an atmosphere much akin to what one found at Zuccotti Park, and throughout the Occupy movement. Occupiers sit, locked in discussion about weighty economic theory or more practical, immediate concerns such as where occupiers will sleep that night, alongside homeless men waging war atop a cheap cloth chess board, playing several feet away from an out-of-town occupier reclined beside the camping rucksack that carries his entire world, not far himself from a suit-clad Wall Street trader, possibly a so-called "one-percenter," who sits quietly enjoying his lunch. Over the course of its first two months in existence, Occupy Wall Street did not just comment on society, it existed within it.

Students and Unions

"Arab Spring, European Summer, American Fall . . ."
—New School students' banner on the march to Foley Square

By the mid-afternoon of October 5, as thousands approached Foley Square for the Community and Labor Rally in solidarity with Occupy Wall Street, a dozen or so graduate students at New York University huddled at the north side of the fountain in Washington Square Park. The sun cast long shadows, as some scribbled slogans on poster board like, "9 of 10 PhDs AGREE MARX WAS RIGHT!" Others leaned against the fountain's edge, sipping coffee and speculating whether anyone would heed their call to walkout, whether the contingent from the nearby New School for Social Research would take the streets. By 4 p.m., however, the square teemed with hundreds of students, professors and community members, and the New School contingent was still on its way.

The NYU organizers had planned for a relatively small contingent of students, marching along the sidewalks to join the community groups and union members downtown. "Because it was just this small number of grad students that organized this thing. We felt like we couldn't in good conscience encourage

NYU undergrads to do something illegal and risk getting arrested," recalled Christy Thorton, an NYU graduate student in history and one of the walkout's organizers, "This was right after the Brooklyn bridge arrests." But as Washington Square swelled with people, a clamor arose north of the park—the New School students had taken Fifth Avenue. As they approached the square's iconic arch, the crowd roared in approval. Daniel Aldana Cohen, a graduate student in sociology at NYU and one of the march's organizers recalled, "When the New School came walking down Fifth Avenue, like down the middle of the street, we were like, all right!" Emboldened, the students set a new goal: occupy the streets.

As the march kicked off, hundreds poured out of Washington Square's southeastern corner. Bearing signs such as "Student Debt = Indentured Servitude," "They Call It Class War Only When We Fight Back!," "Why are so many out of work . . . When there is so much work to be done??," and "We Want Our Future Back," the marchers turned onto the sidewalks along Fourth Street, chanting "We! Are! The 99 percent!" They swarmed around food carts and by the plaza adjoining NYU's Stern School of Business, where several students, some dressed in suits and ties, looked on with light-hearted skepticism. Initially the march stuck to the sidewalks, with only a handful of students walking in the streets alongside traffic. But once they reached Mercer Street, the students flooded Fourth Street. They continued past Broadway, veering right onto Lafayette. Organizers had chosen Lafayette because it had clearer sidewalks than Broadway, which would have been a more symbolic target. "That ended up being an important part of the strategy, because police had no idea," recalled Christy. "They had no idea when we walked past Broadway, they thought where are these people going?"

Clogging two blocks of Lafayette, the marchers brought traffic to a standstill as they headed downtown. Intermittently chanting, "All day! All week! Occupy Wall Street!" and, "One, Two, Three, Four, Wall Street fuck you!" some banged on pots and pans, while others scurried to document the march with their cameras and video equipment. While many in the buildings abutting Lafayette looked on from their windows, many on the ground floor emerged from shops to cheer the marchers on—some even took to the streets in solidarity. As the march approached Worth Street, just north of Foley Square, some New School marchers at the head unfurled a wide paper banner reading, "Arab Spring, European Summer, American Fall . . ." With this message at the fore, the Washington Square feeder march entered Foley chanting "Students! And workers! Shut the city down!" to the cheers of thousands of workers and community members who had already gathered for the subsequent march to Zuccotti.

On October 5, the mass convergence of students and workers at Foley Square, combined with the October 1 arrest of more than 700 OWS protesters on the Brooklyn Bridge, played a pivotal role in raising public awareness of the Occupy movement. The event also shows how Occupy Wall Street facilitated interconnections and coalition building. Indeed, the OWS-enabled solidarity between student and labor movements was by no means inevitable. Conflicting motivations, needs, and goals had in recent years fostered divisions–not only between workers and students, but between students of public and private universities and between workers from different unions. With its amorphous goals, but ardent opposition to budget cuts and corporate takeover of public services, the Occupy movement offered a sufficiently large umbrella to mobilize groups with seemingly disparate priorities toward a common cause. The story of how the October 5 rally and march came to be, and the events it subsequently enabled, highlights Occupy's power as an engine of solidarity.

In May 2011, a group of 25 to 30 student organizers from the

City University of New York and State University of New York
systems met for a lakeside retreat just outside of Albany. Mobilized by state-level threats of budget cuts for higher education
and tuition increases, those gathered formed a coalition called
New York Students Rising (NYSR). Spreading throughout New
York State, the coalition grew from 11 or 12 active campuses
in May to nearly 30 by October. On August 12, NYSR set the
date of October 5 for system-wide walkouts and teach-ins, "in
response to budget cuts, tuition hikes, an absence of administrative accountability, the deterioration of shared governance, and
the troubling threat of privatization." The walkout call came ten
days after the first OWS General Assembly convened in Bowling
Green. According to Colin, an organizer who helped facilitate
NYSR's initial retreat, some members of the burgeoning student
movement had taken part in those early OWS planning sessions
and had tipped off the coalition that a September Wall Street action was in the works. But OWS did not necessarily factor into
the decision to call for a walkout. "Honestly it seemed like a
stretch at the time that [the occupation] could last three weeks,"
Colin said. "The previous model we had for this type of action
was Bloombergville, and it did not last three weeks."

As the occupation of Zuccotti approached its third week,
OWS grew, increasingly collaborating with the burgeoning student movement, and gaining support from labor unions. On
September 29, less than two weeks into the occupation, a coalition of community and labor groups –including United NY,
Strong Economy for All Coalition, the Working Families Party,
the United Federation of Teachers, Workers United, SEIU 1199,
and the Transport Workers Union Local 100—announced they
would hold a Community and Labor Rally in support of Occupy Wall Street the following week, on the same Wednesday
as the NYSR-called student walkout. By October 2, NYSR had
itself endorsed the Community and Labor Rally and October
5 was set as a day of united action by students and workers

in solidarity with the occupiers. The first issue of *The Occu-pied Wall Street Journal*, released on October 1, heralded this unity—its front page displayed a large photo of a pink-haired woman with a tambourine and the headline, "NEW YORK UNITES! WEDNESDAY OCT. 5 STUDENT WALKOUTS UNION MARCHES OCCUPYWALLST.ORG NYSTUDENTSRISING.ORG."

Students and labor did not merely support the Occupy movement, the occupation at Liberty Plaza served as a vital cat-alyst for mobilizing around the distinct causes of students and workers alike. For example, prior to the occupation, and the October 5 call, the student movement in New York had largely been relegated to its public institutions—whose students were directly targeted by state and city austerity measures. But, as Zuccotti bloomed and a wide array of activists intermingled, the occupation united public and private university students and fostered a broader student movement. Josh Frens-String, a graduate student in New York University's history department, said he first heard about NYSR when he was handed a flyer in Zuccotti. Josh, like many other NYU graduate student activists, was a member of the Graduate Student Organizing Committee (GSOC) and had primarily focused his activism on building sup-port for an anticipated union certification vote. But the news of NYSR inspired Josh to build public-private solidarity at NYU. "All that really happened was I posted something to Facebook saying, 'Does anyone know if there's something going on?'— and Dan [DiMaggio] was organizing an NYU walk-out in coor-dination with students at CUNY," Josh said. "So I made my first Facebook group ever for it."

Word of the October 5 solidarity march spread quickly through NYU's departments of History, Sociology, and Social & Cultural Analysis, which are bridged by an intramural soc-cer team called "Historiology" and by GSOC, a United Auto Workers affiliated union of NYU graduate students. GSOC in-corporated the Washington Square feeder march into its phone bank in support of the Community and Labor rally. Other New York City–area university unions—such as the Professional Staff Congress of CUNY–pursued similar efforts. The call also reached the Faculty Democracy list-serve, a list of activist NYU professors. Despite this outreach, those "attending" the march on Facebook numbered around 300, until the official Occupy Wall Street Facebook page promoted the event a couple of days before October 5: then it skyrocketed to nearly 700. Still, those organizing the solidarity march were modest in their expectations. "We thought we were going to get 50 GSOC-affiliated people and we would just wander down there together," recalled Christy Thorton. "But what happened was a giant feeder march and a street takeover." Furthermore, the march congealed a wide group of graduate and undergraduate students under the name NYU Stands with Occupy Wall Street (or NYU4OWS for short)—an organization which, in addition to hosting teach-ins and a recurring People's University in Washington Square Park, mobilized solidarity campaigns around New York's public university students and local workers. More broadly, the October 5 march produced a group called the NYC All-Student Assembly, which facilitated connections among student activists at different universities and helped coordinate broad-based student actions, not only in opposition to cuts in higher education spending and tuition increases, but in solidarity with local workers—especially the art handlers of Sotheby's, Teamsters Local 814. These union members had been locked out of work for failing to agree to an austere new contract, with a 10 percent wage cut and a stipulation granting Sotheby's owners unlimited freedom to hire non-union workers. The latter would have effectively ruined the union.

United together, students and trade unionists affiliated with Occupy Wall Street infiltrated auctions—interrupting the sale of multi-million dollar paintings and furniture. "Sotheby's made record profits of $680 million," one OWS infiltrator would announce in the midst of an auction, "and put its workers out on the street!" Then ten minutes later, after the auction returned to order, a second protester would rise to shout, "the Sotheby's CEO makes $60,000 a day!" This would continue until several had been escorted from the room. These interventions continued, eventually causing Sotheby's to require a $5,000 deposit just to enter the sales room. OWS affiliated protesters also disrupted lunch at high-priced restaurants owned by Danny Meyers, a member of Sotheby's Board of Trustees, informing patrons that the restaurant they were sitting in supported the Sotheby's lockout. The wide array of actions in support of the locked-out Sotheby's workers, which included several arrests for blocking the auction house's doors, culminated on November 9, when 200 people, including Hunter College students and members of at least 10 different unions, joined the Sotheby's picket line.

Indeed, OWS and the burgeoning student movement it fostered provided a lucrative opportunity for the labor movement to stage a broader-based counter-attack against owners' increasingly hard-line tactics at the bargaining table, as well as the renewed threats against collective bargaining in statehouses nationwide. Maida Rosenstein, president of United Auto Workers Local 2110, said, "We in the UAW had been talking about how do we mobilize people and our members not just electronically? How do we mobilize people to get out and protest and rally and demonstrate?" The protests against Wisconsin Governor Scott Walker's attacks on collective bargaining rights in February of 2011, in which students and union workers occupied the State Capitol in Madison before erecting a tent city, served as an important precedent. While they failed to prevent Walker's union-busting law from passing, those protests served to radicalize the labor movement nationwide, and made union leaders quick to recognize the potential benefits of aligning with Occupy Wall Street. "This is a dream come true for us to have these young people speaking out about what's been happening to working people," said George Gresham, president of Local 1199 SEIU, a union of 300,000 health care workers.

Trade unionists were active in Occupy Wall Street from the outset, taking part in the first General Assembly on August 2 and forming the OWS Labor Working Group within the first week of the occupation of Zuccotti. The group, which would come to have more than 100 members representing more than 40 unions, adopted a dual purpose—supporting union struggles and seeking union support for the Occupy movement. By the October 5 rally, the group had succeeded in securing the endorsement of the executive council of the AFL-CIO, the largest federation of unions in the United States. "I was surprised at the eagerness with which the unions responded," said Jackie DiSalvo, a founder of the Labor Working Group. "This alliance is unprecedented in decades in the U.S. and distinguishes Occupy Wall Street from the movements of the '60s when unions were more conservative, and the youth culture tended to be anti-union. The unions have been under attack by the 1 percent, and they're looking for new strategies and new allies."

One such union was Transit Workers Union 100, which in the fall of 2011 was involved in difficult contract negotiations. Working through the OWS Labor Working Group, the TWU rank and file set up a table in Liberty Plaza. Festooned with hard hats left by laborers from the nearby Freedom Tower construction site, the table served as a place where workers could share their stories with visitors to Liberty Plaza, as well as learn about and plug into the movement. The Occupation also facilitated connections among unions. Members of Teamsters Local 802 were introduced to members from Local 814 through the Labor Working group, and the two locals quickly decided to support one another's respective struggles with management. Julian Tysh, an organizer with Local 814, credited the Occupy movement with encouraging workers on picket lines, while universalizing their struggles by pitting them against a common enemy—the 1 percent. "The Occupy movement has changed unions," said Stuart Appelbaum, president of the Retail, Wholesale and Department Store Union (RWDSU). "You're seeing a lot more unions wanting to be aggressive in their messaging and their activity." Indeed, in response to Occupy Wall Street, many unions were quick to seize upon the "99 percent" slogan, affixing it to buttons and signs for the October 5 march.

By 5:30 p.m. on October 5, Foley Square teemed with thousands of students and workers—laughing, chanting, and reveling in the power of their numbers. As the sun set, they trickled out of the square via Centre Street to the south, marching toward Liberty Plaza and the occupation that occasioned their unity. Though the police hadn't restricted the unwieldy feeder march, which had filled two blocks of Lafayette, the NYPD strictly managed the protesters' movements once they entered the square and all along the march to Zuccotti. The contrast could not have been starker. Descending on Foley, the protesters exhibited the unabridged freedoms of speech and assembly that had made the Occupy movement such a breath of fresh air. But as they marched to Zuccotti, police barricades pigeonholed them onto the sidewalk and into one lane of Broadway, while armored officers occupied the rest of the wide avenue. The specter of police authority (and ultimate crackdown) loomed. "What we did marching to Foley Square was an example of the complete opposite," said Josh Frens-String, recalling the contrasting marches. "We took the streets. It was an example of the possible. It was what the march from Foley Square should have looked like—it should have looked like our march, but it didn't. But juxtaposing those two marches—I think it shows where the movement's at and what it's striving for, how much more we're going to have to do."

Living in the Square

"I said, 'I'm a librarian. I can organize books.
At this time, organizing books is a revolutionary act.'"
—Betsy Fagin, volunteer at the People's Library, Zuccotti Park

The Neighborhoods of Zuccotti Park

Occupy Wall Street has acquired notoriety in the press for not having a single message or set of demands, and instead embracing the diversity of opinions that its many different supporters espouse. Various messages were at odds with each other: next to Ron Paul-supporting sworn enemies of the Federal Reserve, who were highly visible holding their "End the Fed" signs along the Broadway side of Liberty Plaza, were others who instead maintained that the Federal Reserve certainly needs reform, but should not be abolished. Zuccotti Park is home to both proponents of specific reforms such as reinstating the Glass-Steagall Act, as well as revolutionaries calling for the complete overthrow of capitalism, or indeed an anarchistic abolition of all hierarchies in American government and society.

As the encampment established itself and evolved in Liberty Plaza, these differences—and eventually, divisions—mapped themselves out on the surface of the square and in the lived experience of those sleeping in the park, particularly after tents began to spring up in late October and early November. Although the divisions were not clear-cut, the square began to divide geographically, creating distinct eastern and western ends.

In many ways, the park was one cohesive whole: despite the variety of ultimate objectives held by OWS's different supporters, everyone involved in the action agreed change was necessary. And in terms of living conditions, with ever more people joining those staying overnight, the entirety of the square soon became crowded and cramped.

It was noticeable, however, that, as the occupation progressed, the eastern and western ends of the square took on an increasingly different aspect from one another. In comparison with the eastern end, where the big red statue was located, the western appeared, on one level, to be more organized: the tents located there were generally larger, providing accommodation for sizeable groups, and they were clustered together in such a way that, starting at the sides of the kitchen, two clear walkways stretched down to the edges of the park.

In contrast with the big sleeping tents at the western end, much of the eastern half of the park was an impassable rat's nest of small single-occupancy tents. Though, here too, parallel walkways existed on either side, they were at points considerably narrower and more twisting than those at the western end. Despite this appearance of packed chaos, the eastern end of the park was home to most of the major organized activities in the square including the media desk, the live feed video center and the library—all of which were housed in large, well sign-posted tents.

Getting into the park was generally straightforward from the eastern end, where a wide swath of steps led down from the Broadway sidewalk to various points of entry. The steps wrapped around the red statue at the south-eastern corner, the site of the People's Stage, and down the square's southern edge;

here too, one could enter unimpeded, save for the occasional protester sitting on the steps or demonstrating in front of them.

It was not so easy to gain access from the western end—a long police barricade blocked off most of it, and myriad protesters sat on the steps that led up into the park, which at this end is elevated from the bordering street, hindering entry. At the south-western corner, a collection of tents blocked a short path, creating a dead end and preventing access to one of the major walkways.

As a result the only route into the park at this end was via the northwestern corner, where a tableau of stark contrast, of a sort unique to Occupy Wall Street, greeted the visitor: just across the road from the tranquility of the meditation space, a raised dais encircling a tree adorned with holders of burning incense and various indeterminable spiritual icons and tchotchkes, loomed the white cantilever of a mobile NYPD observation tower, maintaining a sinister Panopticon stare on the vista below.

But access was only the beginning of the differences between the two ends of the park. Though the distinctions were not hard and fast, west and east ends often *felt* quite distinct, even to the casual visitor. In general it seemed that the eastern end of the park accommodated the more reform-orientated and middle class of the movement's supporters, while the western end housed more working class and politically uncompromising activists.

The eastern end of the park played host to the People's Library, the LBGTQ caucus, Información en Español, and the Press, Media Relations, the Legal working groups and, of course, the General Assembly. It was, in short, where most of the movement's most important functions were headquartered. The western end, by contrast, was home to more overtly radical interventions: a table that advocated taking back land for Native Americans; the Class War Camp, a revolutionary anarchist working group, as well as several other revolutionary booths; and, most famously, the much-maligned drummers of PULSE, who played from a makeshift stage atop the stairs at the western edge of the park.

These were not simply differences in ideological flavoring—they could and did breed a real sense of mutual antipathy between denizens of the eastern and western ends. When describing his organization, KV, one of the organizers of Class War Camp, declared, "This side of the camp isn't for reform. This side's for revolution, you know? We're not—we have nothing to lose. It's not liberal college kids. We don't want to fix the system, we want to fucking burn it to the ground." KV went on to criticize those same "liberal college kids" for returning to sleep in their dorms in the evenings, and recounted how, once, when visiting the eastern end of the park in search of a rumored open mic event, he was told that the event's organizer was away "in the ghetto"—only to discover that "in the ghetto" meant his own end of the park, "near Class War."

The disdain could travel in the other direction too. Daniel Levine, who helped found Info Desk East, the inquiry point that stood at the top of the stairs at the eastern edge of the park, fit KV's characterization of east-end protesters all too well: Levine is a 22-year-old student at Baruch College, who, instead of camping in the park, went home to his apartment in Brooklyn to sleep. Of the western end, Mr. Levine said, "the west end of the park gets pretty nasty sometimes—I'm friends with some of the guys in Sanitation and they tell me that's usually [where it happens] if they have fights or drug dealers," that it was home to "seedier elements," and that the west end was viewed as an undesirable place in which to spend time, because the "drummers, they don't know how to drum. It mostly just sounds like someone knocking on a door really loud for a long time," and because of a maddening concentration there of "fucking hippies who want to play 'The Times They Are A-Changin' 18 times in front of the table." Despite these attitudes Mr. Levine was dismissive of KV's politicized picture of a specifically East-West divide within the park, calling it "an interesting take." Rather, he felt, where people settled in the park was determined not so much by high ideals as, more pragmatically, where the table giving out free cigarettes was located at any given point in time.

Moreover, east versus west was far from the sole axis of division that emerged within the encampment over the course of its first two months. Socio-economic divides in the park became evident around hygiene issues. Middle-class, more educated occupiers tended to have friends, or friends of friends, with apartments not far away. These contacts provided bathing facilities and even beds to crash in when occupiers needed a break from camping. Less schooled, poorer, and more troubled sleepers were, by contrast, left in the cold—even activists from the Comfort working group were not always sure how to help them.

When nearby residents who were sympathetic to the movement offered their apartments for occupiers to shower in, Comfort workers decided to send only those campers whom they felt would be "polite" and "respectful," and who didn't use drugs, to the middle-class households that would be hosting them. Mentally organized people with cultural capital thus had a good chance at getting clean. Others, not so fortunate—perhaps numbering among the western end's "seedier elements"—were less able to get a shower.

The occupation's sleeping areas, too, became marked by differences in class–and race. A young Latino occupier, David, described the Northeast side of the park as full of well-educated and mainly white people, including a sleep camp calling itself the "Upper East Side Sacks." Meanwhile, Zuccotti's Southwest side was "all black and Latino." The divisions were "just like New York City," David noted.

Perhaps most divisive of all was the split of opinion among occupiers concerning the General Assembly and its decisions. Notwithstanding its ostensibly consensus-based structure, the General Assembly was, in the eyes of some, and particularly among residents of the western half of the park, a body that was not truly representative of the totality of the park's round-the-clock occupiers.

Among the GA's detractors along Zuccotti Park's western end, the General Assembly's introduction of large, military-style tents, originally set up to provide a safe sleeping space for women who felt threatened, proved an especially sore point: KV of Class War Camp feared that, despite the tents' original intended purposes, their use would spread and overrun occupiers' existing tents, giving the camp the dreary aspect of a barracks.

An anonymous young woman in her early-to-mid 20s was convinced that a move by the General Assembly that would force occupiers into the military tents was imminent, and expressed serious disquiet at the potential safety hazards she saw in sharing such a tent with a large number of strangers, along with concern about how she would care for her small cat under these conditions. According to her, the General Assembly, moreover, lacked authority to tell occupiers what to do: "Those pussies in the GA don't even sleep here," she accused, "so how can they then turn around and dictate to us who do live here how to live?"

Derrick, another occupier, to whom she expressed these concerns, confirmed that he shared them. Separately, KV also suggested that he, unlike those who participated in the General Assembly, could not attend the nightly meetings because he was busy "holding down [his] camp," and called the Assembly's consensus model "bullshit," because, as he put it, "just because I can't attend . . . doesn't mean I don't have a voice, and if I want to object over there I'd damn well better be able to object right now and say 'fuck you.'" Among these protesters, a sense of revolutionary authenticity was growing, a feeling that not everyone in the Liberty Plaza camp bore the same level of commitment to the protest, and thus, that not everyone had the same right to a voice.

These were only some of the fissures that expanded within

the diverse community residing in Zuccotti. More grievances against the General Assembly came to light. At one point, the assembly's mic checks began to conflict with PULSE's drumming, which led to a dramatic confrontation between the two groups that was ultimately only defused with the help of the movement's corps of mediators. Malfeasance, too, on occasion led to unpleasant episodes, as when Dan Levine discovered that the cigarette-rolling working group, Nick at Nite, was pocketing movement money, leading to the group's disappearance. Occupy Wall Street, an intentionally diverse and inclusive action, was increasingly having to confront divisions that permeated wider society, inside its own ranks.

The Kitchen

If the Zuccotti Park encampment was "semireligious," as *Rolling Stone* magazine said that many in the park described it—and "a spiritual insurrection," according to *Adbusters* editor Micah White, then one of the occupiers' most holy acts was visiting the kitchen to get breakfast, lunch or dinner.

Heather Squire found her calling among the pizza boxes, the peanut butter and jelly, and the lines of OWS sleepers and day trippers, hands outstretched, waiting to be dished up a meal. Arriving at Zuccotti for the first time on October 1, Squire, 31 years old and with a BA in sociology, said she'd spent the four years since graduation filling out applications for entry level jobs sometimes directly, but more often only vaguely, related to her degree. She'd gotten nothing, and her most recent job had been as a $150-a-week deliverer of sandwiches. In the park she recalled that she knew a lot about food: since age 14, she'd worked in restaurants, as a server and in the kitchen. She joined the OWS Kitchen Working Group.

The kitchen lay in the park's center, and in its first weeks it stayed open 24/7, stocked with a glorious hodge-podge of donated food. A middle-aged woman from the Bronx brought a hefty pot of chili. "My husband's in the Transport Workers Union," she said, as though no further explanation was necessary. Others dropped by with fruit, bagels, cookies, hummus, casseroles. Responding to a list of nearby restaurants that delivered, posted on OWS's Web site, the world used its credit cards to purchase take-out for the occupiers. The owner of Liberato's Pizza, near Wall Street, told the *New York Times* he'd received orders from all over the U.S. and from Germany, France, England, Italy and Greece. The Kitchen Working Group's Twitter account buzzed with exclamation marks and thank yous. "Fresh picked apples from Vermont!" enthused one tweet. "Shout out to Nancy in New Mexico for ordering us crazy good food from Katz's Deli!"

In those early days, according to Heather, kitchen workers mostly opened boxes and washed dishes. But the impromptu nature of donations and deliveries made things touch and go. "WE NEED LUNCH!" one Kitchen Working Group tweet entreated. "SEND #OCCUPYWALLSTREET food!" WE'RE HUNGRY!" The occupation began giving the kitchen a budget of up to $1,500 a day for supplementary catering. Some volunteers started cooking in their own, small apartment kitchens. This was necessary because park rules forbade the use of flames to prepare food, and electrical power in Zuccotti was severely restricted.

Farmers helped the Kitchen Working Group to expand its menus. By October, fresh produce was being delivered in trucks dispatched from upstate New York, Western Massachusetts, and Vermont. Small, organic farms and distributors with names like Food Works, Littlewood, and Six Circles were banding together to send harvest to OWS and to the occupation in Boston. They organized a group and named it "Feed the Movement." Emily Curtis-Murphy, of Fair Food Farms in East Calais, Vermont, made a video for Feed the Movement's blog, saying, "Something's got to change," a sentiment felt by many of the farmers providing food to OWS. One of Emily's concerns was that "All this consolidation of wealth isn't doing anything to create jobs for people in the rural economy."

The Zuccotti kitchen staff could slice and dice some farm donations—cucumbers, lettuce, carrots—and make cold salads on site. But Heather wanted to cook the squash, grain and meat, and to use the dairy products without worrying about spoilage. If the kitchen could cook this food, OWS could reduce catering costs and use the savings to reimburse the farmers. Heather began looking for a commercial kitchen with cold and hot storage. Out of the blue, a man named Leo Karl showed up at the information desk.

Leo is pastor of an evangelical church and director of Liberty Café, a soup kitchen in East New York, a poor neighborhood in Brooklyn. Every weekday morning, Liberty Café cooks nutritious, savory lunches for hundreds of poor diners. Leo volunteered to make available the café's huge, well-equipped kitchen in the afternoon, so that OWS could prepare dinner.

Using Liberty Café's facilities, OWS began cooking enormous quantities of food—enough to feed dinner to at least 1,500 people on weekdays, and 3,000 on weekends. The Sustainability Committee helped out with developing a dish washing system, so as to avoid the waste of using disposable plates. The same committee organized a system for getting rid of kitchen scraps, as Brennan Cavanaugh, one of its founders, explained: "With the amount of food that was coming in and the donations and the amount of food being prepared, there was a lot of food waste. It was actually my wife, Catherine's idea to start creating compost buckets and start taking it out. Then it was my idea to start doing it on bicycles."

Cavanaugh and company were soon collaborating with bike activists to form a bike brigade to remove compost. "We have two pickups a day, fourteen a week. Yesterday, we pulled out seven five-gallon buckets of food waste. And we figure those buckets weigh anything from 30 to 35 pounds each. So seven buckets is over two 200 pounds taken out a day." The groups would bring food waste from Zuccotti to community gardens in the Lower East Side, including El Jardin Paraiso, Belinda M'Finda Kalunga Community Garden, La Plaza Cultural, the Lower East Side Ecology Center, and a compost farm called Earth Matter, on Staten Island. "They just make compost and they have chickens. They are a living farm. They come in on their own bike. And they pick up twice a week."

Pedal power was also used to provide electricity for the kitchen, as well as for the rest of the park. "One of the first things we realized we had to do was to get everybody here off of fossil fuels. So we made an energy bike," noted Keegan, of the Sustainability Committee. "Now we can pedal to power a deep cycle battery . . . We started powering some of the things this occupation needs like laptops, cell phones, and cameras. As soon as we plugged it in all the other committees approached us and said we need one too."

Serious foodies were at this point becoming involved in the kitchen. One was Eric Smith, a former chef at Manhattan's Midtown Sheraton hotel. Eric had been laid off, and he volunteered his culinary skills to OWS, as well as his experience cooking for very large groups. Erin Littlestar, meanwhile, had been preparing to be a chef but changed her plans. She told *The Huffington Post* she'd been scheduled to matriculate at the National Gourmet Institute, but never showed up to start classes after she spent a day in Zuccotti. "I just got this feeling like there was something bigger I was supposed to be doing than just going to school to learn chiffonade," Erin said.

The *New York Post,* with typically snide hostility, ran a front page on a "typical" Occupy dinner, prepared in Brooklyn: organic chicken soup with root vegetables, parsley, rosemary and thyme; salad made with sheep's-milk cheese and chimichurri sauce with a dash of garlic; spaghetti; brown rice; beans;

and for dessert nuts and banana chips donated by a co-op in Ithaca.

Mocking the menu as snobbish, the *Post* overlooked two things. For one, the Brooklyn soup kitchen was serving poor people food similar to the OWS menu. And back at Zuccotti, OWS fare went not just to those long-familiar with goat cheese. The kitchen was feeding many far less affluent people. Including the homeless.

By late October, the kitchen working group was feeling overwhelmed by how poorly organized they were relative to the immense job they faced every day. Among the difficulties: a second prep kitchen had opened in Brooklyn, but assigned drivers sometimes didn't show up at either kitchen, so the food sat and spoiled. Heather, and other Kitchen Work Group members, wanted desperately to regroup and fix things.

In late October they decided to take a three-day break to reflect and reorganize during which time they would serve the occupiers only "simplified meals" such as peanut butter and jelly sandwiches. But the kitchen's difficulties got mixed with other problems. Some sexual assaults had occurred in Zuccotti. Drug and alcohol use was becoming more widespread. The Peace Council conferred with Kitchen, suggesting they serve meals for only two hours instead of round the clock, "to discourage people from coming to the camp all fucked up," Heather recalled. When the Kitchen Working Group announced its "simplified" meal plan, on October 27, all hell broke loose. Failing to understand the group's organizational problems, occupiers accused it of trying to starve out the homeless. "People started freaking out," Heather reported. "There was almost violence."

In the end, meal times were restricted, and diners had to stand in a long, snaking line to get their food. After the three-day "simplification," the food returned to being as tasty and healthful as ever. And everyone ate.

At around 4 o'clock in the morning on November 15,

Heather and two co-workers locked arms and sat down on the ground in a puddle of mustard and vinegar that had spilled from bottles smashed by the NYPD during that night's eviction. They had spent their time at the occupation cooking, serving, and washing dishes, then cooking, serving, and washing some more. They were heroes of the kitchen, and perhaps appropriately, the last people in the park to be arrested.

The People's Library

Within days of Zuccotti Park being first occupied, a few dozen books, magazines and pamphlets had been collected by one of the occupiers, a 27-year-old New York University librarian named Jez. He put them on a low wall of the park's northeast perimeter, under a hand-painted sign reading, "Library." A week later, those few dozen books had become hundreds, and by early October, volunteers–some of them professional librarians and some amateurs–were sorting, cataloguing, and marking each new item with a rubber stamp reading, "Occupy Wall Street Library." Soon the library would boast 4,000 books, all donated: everything from *The Essential Chomsky* to *The Letters of Allen Ginsberg* to *He's Just Not that Into You*.

Betsy Fagin, a founding OWS librarian, is a quiet woman

with a halo of dark, curly hair. She lives in Brooklyn and has worked at several libraries, including the National Art Library in London. "I grew up in Washington, DC," Fagin said, explaining how she got involved with the occupation. "My parents went to the MLK march. My father is black, my mother's white. People told them, 'You can't have a child; it's wrong and bad.' I'm here."

Betsy had never been an activist before Occupy Wall Street. Still, she'd had a premonition. "Honestly, it sounds kind of crazy, but I dreamed about this. Not in a conscious way, but literally, years before it happened. And then . . . it did happen."

During the second week of the occupation, she "just got on a train and came over." Immediately she was approached by a young man who invited her to play chess with him. "So we played. The feeling of this place, and how engaging everybody was, and the conversations we had, made me feel, 'This is really important. I can help out here.'"

Looking for a way to make herself useful, Fagin spied the books. "I said, 'I'm a librarian. I can organize books. At this time, organizing books is a revolutionary act.'" She next went to the General Assembly. "'Hi everybody,' I said, a little nervously, 'I'm a librarian and I notice there's a library and nobody's taking charge of it and I'd be happy to if that's cool.' Everybody did the up sparkle finger thing, and that started the library as an official working group."

Soon people began coming to Zuccotti expressly to work in the library. Some even arrived from out of town. One was Mandy Henk, from Greencastle, Indiana, almost 800 miles away. Mandy is a librarian at DePauw University, and she fits the librarian stereotype: she's soft-spoken, bespectacled, and wears her hair pulled back. "I saw Betsy's sign that said the library needed librarians. I'd been waiting for a movement to start for a good long while. So when it did it seemed only appropriate to go ahead and join it."

Mandy made her first trip to OWS the weekend of the Brooklyn Bridge march, and her second on the occasion of her fall break. A third trip soon followed: "It's about a 12-hour trip. We drove the first time with kids and dog in the car, dropped the kids and the dog off at grandma's, and then my husband and I came out. I've flown since then." She brought plastic boxes and tarps to protect books from rain and snow and sleeps in the library when she's visiting. "It's surprising how very similar it actually is to a regular library. The glamour is always in working with the people and not processing the books," she says stamping books with a "People's Library" stamp. "But I think it's great. I think especially when there are professional librarians who can answer the more complex reference questions—we've got legal questions, medical questions, that sort of thing."

Mandy is taking up the cause of Occupy within her profession. "We're presenting at the ALA (the American Library Association). And we get a lot of people visiting the People's Library blog, which I write for. So, more than bringing [Occupy] back to my geographic area, I'm working on communicating with the library profession."

Another out-of-towner, William Scott, is lanky, with a long, studious face. He teaches English at the University of Pittsburgh and was able to volunteer because he was on sabbatical. When interviewed, he noted that his first book was about to be published that very week. He planned to donate it to the People's Library. "It's a dream come true," he said.

Jaime, also a librarian, was proud of the way that Occupation principles were determining how library materials got handled.

"I tell new librarians they can shelve [a book] where they think it goes," Jaime explained. "We don't follow Dewey, we don't follow Library of Congress. If I wander over and don't think it goes there, I'll put it somewhere else. Direct democracy. If something can go in economics or in women or history,

I'll say, "For this particular work, where do I think people will be most happy to find it?" The principle of use says, "Is this the way readers are actually going to use these books?" Certain novels should be shelved in [Young Adult] because every teenage girl I've known has found it to be their first exposure to erotica, even though it's an adult novel –because the use is by teenage girls. They'll be the ones happy to find it. If you put it in general fiction, no one will ever read it."

The library working group created a poetry anthology, and worked in solidarity other actions around the country. "We've sent out stuff to other occupations," Jaime said, "including to Philadelphia and Detroit." The group also created a blog that contains a search engine for every book the librarians were able to catalogue and stamp. That wasn't every item because sometimes people took books just as they came in, and never brought them back.

"Our circulation policy is, basically, if you want it and you feel like you need it in your heart, then take it. We ask that you leave a trade or bring it back," Betsy explained. "The cynic in me is saying you can't just give this away for free." She recalled the time when someone came to the occupation library from a store that buys used books. He said he'd been getting a lot of books from people who'd taken them from the People's Library and wanted to sell them. "My heart sank a little," Fagin remembered. "But then somebody said, 'If they're selling the books they probably need the money.' And the bookstore guy said, 'We're taking the books and bringing them back to you.'"

The librarians were frequently busy with reference chores. "People come in and are like, 'I'm looking for something about renewable energy,' and we're finding the books and getting them information," Betsy said. But all was not work. "Authors come through to donate their books and hang out and talk. Scott was thrilled when Angela Davis visited. So did Philip Levine, current poet laureate of the United States. He left one of his books, signed. The not-so-famous came, too, of course: "to chill out and to read and to think and to engage with each other and with the world, with all of human experience," Betsy said. To her, the library was "the heart" of the community.

"This is a paradigm shift," Betsy again, talking of everything going on in Zuccotti Park. "It's the beginning—it's not even the beginning, it's been going on. But it's accelerating. I just love it, and part of what I like is stamping the books so it says 'Occupy Wall Street Library.'"

Not long after Betsy and her fellow workers were interviewed for this book, everyone and everything was evicted from Zuccotti Park. Of the 4,000 books tossed by police into garbage trucks and carted away, only 839 were recovered in usable condition from a city sanitation warehouse. A few others were found damaged beyond use from their trip in the trucks. The rest, over 3,000 items donated to the People's Library, simply disappeared.

Legal

Occupy Wall Street is, at its heart, a movement rooted in the tradition of civil disobedience. Symbolic actions, often technically illegal, are the hallmark of a movement that started by claiming space for itself, with no permission sought, in the very center of world capitalism. In such a movement, legal counsel was likely to prove constantly necessary, and indeed it has: the frequency with which the movement has had to engage in legal struggles, both on the individual and the institutional level, convinced attorney and OWS participant Janos Marton of the necessity, as he put it, for Occupy Wall Street to keep its lawyers "in the loop" as much as possible. While perhaps less visible than the kitchens or the medical tent, the New York Occupy encampment, since its first weeks, boasted a working group dedicated to legal support, an activity that remained a vital part of life in Zuccotti throughout the occupation.

Janos, an attorney on the New York Bar, was an early member of the Legal working group. He heard about the Occupy Wall Street initiative before September 17 by way of *Adbusters*, but was only able to visit Zuccotti for the first time two days after the occupation began. Though initially thwarted by the non-hierarchical nature of OWS in his attempts to locate a contact person for the legal working group—there was no clear, single coordinator with whom to speak—by the second week of the occupation, and after a brief stint working in the People's Library, he found what he was looking for. One evening in late September, at a coffee shop close to Zuccotti, he attended the second meeting of the recently-formed Legal working group.

"We try to meet weekly, and there's always a pressing issue," Janos said of the working group. The pressing issue at that first meeting he attended would remain a constant concern for Legal throughout the occupation—that of jail support. A serious problem facing the movement's legal wing in its earliest days, Janos recalled, was that of getting lawyers access to arrested protesters: no police officer would simply grant cell access to a lawyer who presented herself at a precinct, armed only with the claim that she represented arrested protesters in police custody—full, legal names are a basic requirement for access to arrestees.

When, at the General Assembly a few days prior, on September 23, a call had gone out on the People's Mic asking lawyers to volunteer to go help arrested protesters languishing in NYPD cells, Janos discovered that no one knew the names of any of the jailed individuals, and as a result, found himself unable to do anything to help them.

The meeting in the coffee shop had to resolve this issue and did so by setting up the jail support subgroup, charged with organizing and providing material as well as legal support for arrested OWS protesters. The meeting also created a lawyer relations subgroup, tasked with liaising with the Occupy Wall Street movement's principal source of legal support, the National Lawyers' Guild. One of its responsibilities was that of collecting and passing along the names of arrested OWS supporters.

The National Lawyers' Guild has been the center of the Occupy Wall Street movement's legal structure. It is a national organization of progressive and radical lawyers, with a long history of providing legal support to protests, particularly through its Legal Observers program. This program trains individuals on how to best observe a protest, taking good notes, so that potential arrests can be handled smoothly. Outfitted with highly visible neon-green Legal Observer baseball caps, National Lawyers' Guild members have been a visible presence at every sizeable OWS action, keeping watch for any instances of police misconduct and taking down the names of arrested protesters. By the end of October the Guild had approximately 20 attorneys working on legal research and litigating on behalf of Occupy Wall Street.

Soon after its creation, the legal working group set up a table in Zuccotti. A legal support table already existed at the time, run by the National Lawyer's Guild, but it was staffed only from 5 p.m. to 7 p.m. limiting its usefulness. For three days, Janos took time off from the New York City law firm where he works to staff the working group's new table, located beside the Media Relations station in the park's north-east corner. Over the course of those three days, he listened to one heartbreaking story after another. Most, for instance those relating to home foreclosures, lay beyond the purview of the working group and Janos often found himself in the difficult position of being unable to do anything. On other occasions, however, especially on matters concerning arrests during protest actions, he was able to help.

By late October, Occupy Wall Street's legal support structure had expanded, from an initial corps of around 10 in late

September, to a total strength of 22 volunteers a month later, with perhaps 15 arguing cases at any one time. The lime-green caps of the National Lawyer's Guild Legal Observers could be observed at virtually every major protest that the Occupy movement staged. On the actions of October 14, for example, they were present both in Zuccotti Park and at the marches on City Hall and Wall Street. On the latter march, one Legal Observer was run over by an NYPD scooter, an incident that was caught on film and rapidly gained notoriety on the Internet. Writing the Guild phone number on one's forearm, and using it to contact the Guild after being arrested, became standard practice for protesters.

The legal working group's relationship to the rest of the movement also evolved. Janos explained how: before October 20, the process by which individuals could take legal action on behalf of Occupy Wall Street was not well-organized. This sometimes resulted in ill-considered legal motions being filed on behalf of the movement that the General Assembly did not in fact support, and which could even prove embarrassing or damaging to OWS.

On October 20, the General Assembly passed a motion—which Janos supported—that required any legislation affecting the OWS community as a whole to be previously submitted to the GA for approval. This new system was not perfect, Janos acknowledged. At times, as he put it, legal matters require "fast turn-around," to which the procedures of the General Assembly approval were not conducive, So, for example, while the National Lawyers' Guild had sent the New York Fire Department a legally charged letter in late October in response to the FDNY's removal of power generators from Zuccotti, moving forward with actual litigation still awaited General Assembly approval at the end of the encampment in mid-November. But overall, Janos considered the balancing act between efficiency and organization to be generally successful. On November 15, when Mayor

Bloomberg at last sent in the NYPD to evict the OWS camp, the NLG responded by filing a restraining order.

The Media Center

Whether it was reporters from NY1, New York City's local news channel, or journalists working for foreign news agencies such as the BBC, Spain's La Sexta, or Al Jazeera, the Occupy Wall Street encampment found itself from its first days the target of frequent visits by members of the press. With journalists came questions—quickly, the Occupy movement realized it had need of articulate, informed supporters able to liaise with the press, answering the many questions that arose about a hard-to-categorize, leaderless, and ostensibly demand-less uprising. As a result, the Occupy movement moved early on to put together a Press Relations working group - designated occupiers armed with information about the movement and drawn from within its ranks - in the hope of communicating at least some truth about the encampment at Zuccotti through a media often characterized by misrepresentation and confusion.

Press Relations set its table up in the north eastern quarter of the park, amid a cluster of the most visible and important groups, including the People's Library and the Legal working group. Mark Bray and Senia Barragán were two early members of the working group. Longtime activists and self-professed anarchists, the pair, who in daily life are History Ph.D. students, began participating in the Occupy movement from its first day, when, having learned of the occupation plans through Facebook, they joined OWS's inaugural September 17 march on Wall Street. For Senia, in particular, joining Occupy Wall Street was not just about political belief, it was personal too. As she explained, her support for the movement was spurred by an occasion when her family's home was nearly foreclosed upon as a result of a single late mortgage payment. Mark, meanwhile, felt he could best serve the movement by using the public speaking skills he had acquired teaching history to relay clear messages to the media.

As part of the Press Relations group, press interviews did, in fact, feature from the beginning as an important portion of both Mark and Sennia's duties, so much so that they felt they could not camp in the park like other OWS participants. Serving as a representative of the movement before the press meant that they had to turn out every day well-groomed and dressed in clean clothing, which necessitated returning each evening to their apartment in Jersey City, NJ.

Interviews for the Press team were frequent—three per day, every day, by one estimate—and were with, as another member of the group, Jason Ahmadi described as "[the greatest] variety of journalists I've seen in my life," spanning "everything you can possibly imagine." One of the more high profile exchanges took place on October 16 when Mark participated in an interview with Al Jazeera, in which he exchanged opinions with independent stock trader Alessio Rastani, and offered a straightforward, two-part explanation of what the Occupy Wall Street movement sought: economic justice, and a more democratic, accountable form of politics that was beholden to citizens rather than to corporations.

Four days earlier, he had suggested to an interviewer from CNN Money that those who criticized the movement for lacking demands were missing the point—OWS was seeking a conversation about the current state of the country, not presenting a finite list of goals. "Making a list of three or four demands," he asserted, "would have ended the conversation before it started."

On November 14, the day before the NYPD eviction, Mark was again in the news, this time speaking to the progressive journalism Web site Nation of Change, discussing why he foresaw that Occupy Wall Street would not consent to align itself with any existing political party. When occupiers were at last temporarily evicted from Zuccotti Park on November 15, Mark spent the early morning hours between roughly 1 a.m., when the eviction took place, and sunrise, shuttling back and forth between his New Jersey apartment and Zuccotti, talking to the news teams that had parked their vans along the street along the southern edge of the park. The following day he held a telephone interview with *Bloomberg Businessweek*, during which he refuted the assertion, made by AIG Chairman Steve Miller, that OWS protesters held "unsophisticated" views on the relationship between Wall Street and broader, "Main Street," prosperity in America.

Senia Barragán, meanwhile, had no shortage of interviews herself, though due to family obligations, she could not come to Zuccotti Park daily. In the wake of Occupy Wall Street's successful October 14 standoff with Brookfield Properties, she spoke with Al Jazeera, calling Brookfield Properties' retreat a "big victory" for the Occupy movement, and told *Time* Magazine that, " . . . this was never about sanitation. It was about a pretext for eviction." One month later, in her capacity as an OWS spokeswoman, she spoke to NBC New York on the morning of the November 17 Day of Action, as protesters attempted to block entry onto Wall Street, as well as with the South African Broadcasting Corporation.

In addition to interviews, Senia was also busy with a Press Relations working group project to create a list of spokespeople drawn from Occupy Wall Street's various minority groups. In this way the Press team hoped to increase its own diversity and bring more underrepresented voices into contact with the media covering OWS. At first, she explained, the Press team had been overwhelmingly white and male, something that ran counter to Occupy Wall Street's practice of privileging the voices of historically disenfranchised and persecuted groups. Senia, of Colombian heritage, was, she recalled, the first person of color involved with Press Relations, and had, at first, not been taken seriously by members of the Press, though she made a special effort to dress professionally. She explained that the working group had grown markedly more diverse as a result of an ongoing effort to bring in new people, and the list of minority spokespersons was only growing.

The sort of questions and answers that Press team members such as Barragán, Bray, and Ahmadi offered in these interviews were reflective of the horizontal, demand-less nature of the movement. Many of the Press team's answers were descriptive, rather than presenting an analysis of the movement. They steered members of the press toward Occupy participants from whom they could get the specific answers they wanted, or answered questions about the movement themselves, but were careful not to phrase their own expectations of the movement, their own goals, as things that the movement as a whole embraced. As Press team member Jason put it, in situations where "messaging" questions come up in press interviews—questions about the message of the movement, its goals or expectations for the future— "we are very clear about saying 'I' statements: using 'I believe this,' 'I want,' 'these are my goals.'" Most commonly, the questions press team members received were ones like, "When are you leaving?" "What are you going to do for the winter?" "What are your goals?" and, similarly, "Why are you here?" However, on occasion, some outlandish and off-topic issues also came up, as when one journalist asked Jason about his love life. This particular question was a point of pride for Ahmadi, as he, by his own reckoning, "flipped the question on her," moving the conversation to her relationship with a physician who had children, and her opinion that there were no good men to date in New York City.

Press relations, however, was just one dimension of a larger and ongoing project —that of reaching out and spreading the message of OWS to the public beyond the park. Another, perhaps unlikely collaborator in increasing the transparency of the movement and connecting outsiders with events transpiring inside was a 27-year-old Twitter user, a man, who went by the handle DiceyTroop, and was responsible for providing live, real-time reports via Twitter of the business being handled at Occupy Wall Street's nightly General Assembly meetings.

As was the case for Senia, DiceyTroop's motives for first getting involved with Occupy Wall Street were personal as well as political, rooted in his own biography: a native of Foxboro, Massachusetts, he had been raised in the Unitarian Universalist church, and as a young man had helped organize a radical youth organization within the church that had, among other measures, embraced the consensus model of discussion and decision-making. When DiceyTroop first witnessed a General Assembly, his brain, as he put it, "exploded"—here were hundreds successfully using the consensus model outside and in public, when he had only ever seen it operating in "enclosed radical cirles."

Fascinated, he tweeted a report of the General Assembly that evening on his regular Twitter account, only to have the main OWS Twitter account, and then 70 other accounts, retweet it. Realizing the need he had discovered—no record of the General Assembly's proceedings had to that point existed on Twitter—he returned the next night to live-tweet the whole event. He continued to do this for several weeks until, made uncomfortable by the number of Twitter followers that DiceyTroop as an individual had acquired, followers that according to him "really belonged to the movement," he helped build a "Twitter Team" that has since taken over live-tweeting GA business under the collective handle LibertySquareGA.

Meditation Space

At the intersection of Liberty and Trinity, a few paces into the northwest corner of Liberty Square, stands a tree surrounded by low granite benches. These benches form a ring around the tree, making it the focal point of the seating area. The tree is a London plane, a hybrid species that resulted from the combination of an oriental plane and the American sycamore. Most trees within the city parks of New York are peculiar reminders of the concrete jungle that surrounds them; there's nothing natural about a tree emerging from polished granite. Yet this hybridized flora was one of the focal points of the OWS encampment at Liberty Square. Away from the hustle and bustle of the assembly area, the kitchen, and the dozens of other working groups, the Tree of Life (as it was renamed by the occupants) became the spiritual center of the park. There was an earlier testament to its significance too: the tree survived the collapse of the World Trade Center just a block away on 9/11.

In the weeks prior to the occupation of Zuccotti Park, members of Meditation Flash Mob (MedMob for short), a holistic community that has been producing events in the NYC area for years, meditated on Wall Street outside the NY Stock Exchange. They also held public meditations at Union Square and Washington Square Park. Anthony Whitehurst, a member of Med-Mob, described the collective as a collaborative effort of many individuals, with about 10–12 active facilitators in the group. He added that MedMob's structure is intended to be universal: "It includes chanting the sound of ohm, silent meditation, and playing music." Following a Flash Mob meditation on October 5, members of MedMob and the Consciousness Working group, among other groups in the community, created the beginnings of the community altar. Charlie Gonzalez, a founder of the Consciousness Group, created a sign declaring the London plane as the "Tree of Life, a community sacred space." Within a few days, the space began to flourish.

The Sacred Space, as it is designated on the map of Zuccotti Park, was used for self-reflection, yoga, chanting, prayer, and meetings with a spiritual focus. When speaking to the participants involved in the creation of the space, they made clear that it was not owned or defined by any one group. Rather, as Charlie put it, it was "a collective shared space that many different groups can work with in their own ways, and all of whom will have their own views and opinions."

The initial altar at the Tree of Life was handmade and donated by an OWS supporter. Occupier and New York native Michael Rodriguez was often to be found at the tree. He built a second altar, and both he and Brendan Butler, another member of the Consciousness group, looked after its general upkeep and design for most of the days that it was up. Rodriguez and Butler were often referred to as the guardians of the altar. It was around this altar that members of the public and the Occupy Wellness Group (including MedMob, Occupy Yoga, the Interdependence Project, and other groups) organized and maintained 58 days of continuous prayer, twice daily meditation, music, interfaith practices, worship, and community discussions. Occupiers and visitors alike contributed a myriad of objects to the altar: sage, flowers, candles, Buddha statues, Hindu deities, Day of the Dead decorations, peace signs, crucifixes, Balinese masks, rosaries, rose petals, malas, stones, feathers, shells, crystals, incense, candles, figurines, Buddhas, photos of spiritual teachers, signs and art work.

In the daily life of OWS, the Sacred Space offered a refuge from crowds and chaos, a place for occupiers to pause and reflect on their feelings and priorities. The benches also provide a place for tired tourists and visitors to sit and interact with occupiers. On October 28, Brendan, created a Facebook page for the Tree of Life. On its page, the tree is described as "A community altar and sacred space dedicated to unifying the 100%." Fateh Singh of Occupy Yoga added that it "served as a symbol—a real touchstone—for those who believed in something greater than themselves. In that way, it was perfect a spiritual centerpiece of the Occupy Movement, and a material representation of awareness." One or two weddings were even conducted at the Tree of Life, a testament to its place in the movement. Charlie commented, "The beauty of the 'Tree of Life' concept is that it is not from one religion or dogma, but is prevalent in all traditions, and even science, as a symbol of our interconnectedness."

It was significant that the Tree of Life stood within view of the new One WTC tower, and only a few blocks from the 9/11 Memorial. Though this was sometimes forgotten in the commotion of the Square, Lisa Montanarelli, a facilitator of the Meditation Group, found that people often commented on it in the discussions following meditation sessions. The 9/11 attacks on the World Trade Center were also seen as anti-capitalist protests, targeting the symbols of U.S. economic might. Those who recognized this correlation believed that the memory of the attacks made OWS more consciously nonviolent and inclusive of religious diversity. While 9/11 was often framed as a religious war between Christians and Muslims, or a "clash of civilizations" between the Euro-American West and the Arab world, OWS traced its roots to the Arab Spring and promoted solidarity with similar anti-corporate protests worldwide, regardless of national borders or religious differences.

As the occupation developed, the Consciousness Group grew, drawing in members from MedMob and many other organizations. The working group promoted a variety of activities including a spirit-based women's circle, a men's circle, Angel Walks, Meditation, Individual Energy Healings, non-violent communication to police, and Channeling and Spiritual Warrior Work. As its larger mission, the group supported events and ideas that promoted raising group consciousness at Occupy Wall Street. According to its members, this was why the activities of the group had such range and variety.

The Wellness Working Group emerged from the efforts of individuals like Fateh Singh of Occupy Yoga, who tried to get all the groups to work together. The group had organized only a few meetings when the park was evicted. It was an inclusive, unifying group that emphasized mindfulness. The Interdependence Project, a nonprofit with a secular approach to Buddhist meditation, launched its daily meditations on October 18. In particular, Adreanna Limbach of the Interdependence Project put great effort into organizing the daily sits and creating the Meditation Working Group. The Interdependence Project works to cultivate an understanding of the connection between personal transformation practices and social transformation through ongoing workshops related to Art, Activism, Meditation and Buddhist Philosophy & Western Psychology. The group's meetings included Buddhists from a variety of traditions, and secular mindfulness practitioners. The meetings were likely more diverse, but the group didn't ask about spirituality or religious affiliations.

Members of the Wellness Group continue to speak about how they might introduce secular mindfulness practices into the GA meetings and working group procedures–to facilitate non-violent communication, deep listening, and compassion for oneself and others. One of the goals of the group was to provide a space for people to confront existing differences, rather than suppress them. The Meditation sessions put individuals in touch with their responses to particular issues in a non-violent, non-confrontational setting. This avoided immediate reactions, which were often based on misunderstanding and could lead to larger disagreements.

The daily meditations were small, but evidently beneficial. The Meditation Working Group offered hour-long sessions every weekday from 3:30 to 4:30 and weekends from 1:00 to 2:00. The meditation facilitators came from two groups: the Interdependence Project and MedMob. The daytime facilitators rotated daily, and the meditations often included walking meditation and seated guided meditation. Facilitators provided instruction beginning with shamatha, (which involved bringing awareness to the breath, noticing when the mind wandered, and bringing it back) and a lovingkindness meditation (where participants started with love for themselves and loved ones and gradually expanded outward to include all beings).

Well-known individuals within the New York spiritual community supported the meditations at Zuccotti. The Meditation group coordinated public speaking appearances by Robert Thurman, founder of Tibet House; Russell Simmons participated in one of the group meditation circles; and Deepak Chopra led a group meditation at the square. The most common feedback facilitators heard was that the meditation helped participants gain distance from strong emotions; they had a choice whether or not to act upon their anger, for instance. On several occasions, one of the participants had been ready to attack another protestor at their next working group meeting and decided, after the meditation, to approach them more empathically instead.

Additionally, MedMob offered silent meditations as opposed to facilitated classes. Charlie Gonzalez described his role outside the MedMob meditations: "Most of the time I floated around the park to de-escalate different situations, talk with people individually to practice active listening and share ideas, and to remind everyone that we are already free and we do not need to demand anything from anyone to realize our own liberation. I was not there to protest. I was there to co-create a new world." Charlie had noticed a global shift in consciousness; that is, people were starting to realize they were not as alienated as they believed, but part of a larger interconnectedness.

John Paul Learn, also a MedMob member, emphasized the role of group meditations in attracting individuals to participate in OWS: "the group meditations showed an intention and action that went beyond non-violence and truly embraced and embodied compassion." At their largest, group meditations involved over 200 people, all focusing their "altruistic attention in a communal area, seemingly non-religious or non-spiritual in its actual physical makeup, and showing that locations and the people in them can literally be transformed into a sacred space . . . if we allow ourselves to do so," Learn said. In their words, meditation was a form of indirect action.

Following some of the Meditation sessions, facilitators led group discussions that addressed healthy approaches to handling the various challenges the occupation presented. After a particular session, Lisa Montanarelli recalled hearing a reference to the "Upper East Side Sacks." The individual who said this was referring to the class divides that had emerged in the park. Lisa had just led a Buddhist lovingkindness meditation, which involved visualizing someone who was difficult or challenging and extending love to that person. Afterward, as the participants discussed anger, a young Latino occupier named David brought up how conflict between the "Haves" and "Have-nots" had spread throughout the park: "If you look at the south[east] side of the park, they're all white and educated. There's one sleep camp—they call themselves the 'Upper East Side Sacks.' There are few people of color sleeping on the south side, but they're educated too. Meanwhile, the north[west] is all black and Latino. It's just like New York City."

The group then spoke about how OWS was an effort to create a community where people took care of (and cared about) each other, but everyone needed to change themselves so they didn't replicate the same class and racial hierarchies that exist in the society from which they came. Sia, a black woman in her early twenties, said, "We can create a different structure on the outside of things, but unless we change the view from inside, nothing actually changes."

Occupy Yoga also played a role in the life of the sacred space. A group of Kundalini Yoga teachers began leading nightly yoga classes in Zuccotti Park on October 11 a class which debuted with 100 yogi participants, and, at the time of writing, has been there every night since. It offered Kundalini Yoga meditation classes from 6–7p.m. around the Tree Of Life. The group was founded by Fateh Singh and Hari Simran Khalsa, but worked with a rotation of teachers, including several elder teachers—both local and out of state—who had studied directly with Yogi Bhajan. Some teachers, like accomplished musical guest yogi Sat Kartar Kaur, came from as far away as California, just to lead a single night class and serve the Occupy Movement.

On some rainy days, members of the movement incorporated creative actions, like serving food, tea or helping clean the camp, to help facilitate the goals of unity and peaceful protest. Occupants recalled seeing yogis leading the active meditative practice in the square, where the participants and visitors alike rolled out their mats, or stood around the group and followed along. Fateh Sigh described his experience of the nightly classes: "We had 30–40 people every night and we always had classes in the circle, and in the circle everyone was welcome who wanted to join in."

After the eviction on November 15, Michael Rodriguez, Brendan Butler and Charlie Gonzalez went to the sanitation facility and retrieved one tattered Quan Yin statue. Everything else seemed to have been destroyed, including three relics (one of them a large Tibetan thangka and a mask from Bali). Charlie suggested that group members put together a protest petition that the whole group could get behind, and reach out to spiritual leaders of all wisdom traditions to sign the document. He also proposed that the Consciousness Group invite leaders in the community to come out to hold a press conference and event to rebuild the altar. For many people, the objects destroyed were sacred. Fateh Singh characterized the destruction of the altar as "the disrespect of people's religious freedom to express themselves." It was proposed by Charlie that the Consciousness Group take legal action regarding the desecration of the altar. "Our goal is to re-establish a setting for us to maintain a sacred space for the open public. We hope to have a way of gathering the spirit of all religious and faith-based approaches—to congregate, build community and improve our human relationships moving collectively towards a better future," Singh said.

Rebeka Beiber, who has been participating since the second week of OWS with MedMob, the Consciousness Group and lately the Meditation Working Group, added that "with the eviction comes a practice of non-attachment and a shift from attachment to 'place' and a greater focus on creativity." Those participating, organizing and facilitating the within the larger Wellness Group seemed to understand that the integration of past, present and future was essential to their process. This connectivity resulted from the group's fundamental belief that a peace-full person first, a peace-full collective second leads to a peace-full earth. "What is remarkable about OWS is just how quickly we adapt and HOW we are adapting," Beiber said.

To those involved in the Consciousness Group, and the OWS movement in general, the Tree of Life was a direct expression of the people's collective spiritual intentions and right to Freedom of Religion. It was an inclusive, open, and collaborative creation, made from hundreds of individual's donations, time, and effort. It became a peaceful meeting space for reflection and prayer from its humble beginnings, and was a place of solace and quietude within the plaza. John Paul Learn expressed that "these actions helped to create a more participatory, inclusive environment within the movement and helped to broaden the scope of the voices being heard."

Medic tent

As soon as the occupation of Zuccotti Park got underway, a small and dedicated group of street medics emerged to look after the health of the protesters. Street medics have been a part of protest culture since the Civil Rights movement of the mid-sixties, when protesters discovered that a sympathetic medical presence was indispensable to their cause. It was evident then that protesters facing police brutality could not expect an adequate medical response from authorities. The protesters a half decade ago also found that, as the 1966 Orientation Manuel for the Medical Committee for Human Rights (one of the first voluntary activist medical groups) put it, "actual violence seems to occur less often if it is known that medical professionals are present." Loosely organized and locally autonomous, street medics became an indispensable part of the tradition of American dissent. They were very active in protests against the Vietnam War, in the American Indian Movement, in the Black Panther party, and a wide range of political dissent in the latter 20th century. Tom Hayden, the Students for Democratic Society activist who has trained as a medic, explained that "there was a need for an alternative to hospitals. The police would go to hospitals looking for fugitives to arrest."

Previous to Occupy Wall Street, the defining moment of latter day street medicine was the protests against the WTO in Seattle in 1999. In the wake of those protests, medics organized collectives and began to train more people to offer medical treatment in crisis situations. These collectives have had a largely unacknowledged role in many major events. They were represented on the flotilla carrying humanitarian aid to Gaza in May 2010 when Israel killed nine activists. They have established permanent clinics in New Orleans and in other areas underserved by the established system.

The animating belief of street medicine is that medical care is a human right, and should be freely and immediately available to everyone. Some of the medics who formed the core of the team at Zuccotti Park, including Pauly Kostora, were the most dedicated caregivers in the wake of the hurricanes and earthquake in Haiti. Pauly told me that experience gave him a sense of perspective and scale that made his work in Zuccotti Park seem, in contrast, quite straightforward.

On September 17, Pauly and a handful of other medics were on hand at the beginning of the occupation, armed with only basic supplies–bandages, disinfectant, gauze. They were the only part of the occupation that had to be active and in service 24 hours a day, and so were happy to accept offers of help from anyone who wanted to be involved. Breanna Lembitz, a 21-year-old who joined the occupation a few days later and who subsequently became deeply involved in other aspects of the movement, remembered with fondness her first day with the medical team: "They had three arrests that day, and they worried they wouldn't have enough manpower if everyone kept getting arrested. At that point it was me, one other girl, Lily [Johnson] and six other guys. So it was like me and a bunch of brothers."

The medic area was the first location in the park to be blocked off from the rest of the community's space, a move that caused some contention among the egalitarian-minded protesters. But having a dedicated area to treat and support the community's health became a foundation of the occupation at Liberty Park.

On September 23, the medic team put out a call to action for medics around the country, and qualified medical professionals streamed in to the square to help. Among those who answered the call was Ed Mortimer, who became the point person for drug and alcohol interventions, and Frank White, a mental health specialist. They told me how they felt inspired by the wide support the medic team received. They had the regular assistance of licensed doctors and nurses, some of whom took time off from their work at hospitals such as the Woodhull Hospital and who were able to write needed prescriptions in the park itself. "Everyone works to their own qualifications," explained Miriam Rocek, another member of the medic team.

Medics have a different role in marches and direct actions than the protesters. They are to remain neutral. Although the medical tent sports a banner that demands free healthcare for all, because, as Pauly said, "that's our issue," when medics don the red or red-and-black crosses that differentiate themselves from protesters, they assume the responsibility to provide immediate medical care for anyone around them who needs it, whether they are protester, cop, or bystander. They can also act as neutral observers of the action–Ed told me that on the strength of his status as a medic during the mass arrests on the Brooklyn Bridge, he was able to push past the first cordon of police officers to closely observe the arrests and ensure that the protesters were not abused.

Near 11:30 at night on Monday, October 10, a police lieutenant roughly woke up Ed Mortimer while he slept right next to the medical tent. The police were mobilizing to confiscate the tent. As the cops moved in, medics and protesters formed a human chain around the area. As his arms locked with his comrades, Ed looked to his left and saw Jesse Jackson clambering over a flowerbed to join in. Jackson locked arms with the protesters, saying, "I'm not visiting, I'm occupying." Seeing the determination of the movement to maintain its medical facilities, the police backed down and dispersed.

Medics have been essential in caring for injuries resulting from police brutality. Street medics have developed an effective treatment for pepper spray: antacid mixed with water, which has saved people's eyesight. One medic described patching up a protester who was caught in a crowd panicked by the police's use of teargas, another stitched up wounds incurred at the wrong end of a police baton.

Along with hypothermia and trenchfoot (stinkfoot), one of the central problems that the medic team faced in the park itself was the issue of mental health. Breanna described one man's psychic breakdown in detail: he hadn't slept in days due to the drumming, and he thought that her soothing hand was killing him by stealing what remained of his energy. The medic team comforted him, and eventually got him to sleep - the man quickly became integrated into the community as a member of the sustainability committee. Pauly explained to one reporter, "The distress of sleeping on the street and experiencing sleep deprivation can lead to a whole series of medical issues."

But not all of the mental health and addiction issues that the medical team confronted in the park were a product of the occupation itself. As Frank put it to me, the protesters "are fighting against a system that has been beating them down all their lives, and that can lead to emotional problems." In a series of ways, the medic team was mopping up after a broken society and a broken healthcare system.

Many protesters in Zuccotti saw the presence of free and open healthcare in the park as a living reinforcement to their political positions; the fact that they would provide a service that was utterly lacking in the society at large was a visceral indictment of capitalism and for-profit healthcare. Maria Fehling, a nurse with National Nurses United, said, "We see a lot of people who otherwise have not sought out healthcare in five, six years because they have no insurance."

When the NYPD raided the encampment in the early hours November 15, they confiscated a vast quantity of the medical supplies the team had stockpiled over the course of the occupation. The medics were left with what they started: the most basic supplies that they could carry on their person. They tried to reclaim anything they could from the NYPD, but the police had destroyed their two defibrillator units and any other equipment that was breakable. Nonetheless, the medics continue to evolve with the movement, fully committed. "I'm cold, wet and invisible," Ed said, "but it's the best time of my life."

Defending the Occupation

*"You guys are not going to get much sleep tonight.
We're going to clean up all night . . . we need more coffee."*
—A broom-wielding occupier in Zuccotti Park

On the evening of October 12, 2011, Zuccotti Park received an unexpected visitor. Mayor Michael Bloomberg, who two days earlier had declared that he would not evict Occupy Wall Street so long as it broke no laws, arrived at the park to shake the hands of Occupiers and to vow that he would balance their First Amendment right to assemble with the rights of other New Yorkers and Brookfield Properties, the park's owners.

By the next morning, the city's tone seemed to shift. Just after 8 a.m. on October 13, a line of police officers, armed with stacks of paper, marched through Zuccotti. They passed out a notice from Brookfield Properties announcing a planned cleaning of the park at 7 a.m. the following day, October 14, and a new set of park rules. Under the new rules the use of tarps and sleeping bags was expressly prohibited, as were tents. The notice also banned "lying down on the ground, or laying down on benches, sitting areas, or walkways which unreasonably interferes with the use of benches, sitting areas, or walkways by others." The signal was clear—the occupation was being declared illegal. Upon reading the notice, occupier Mesiah Burciaga-Hameed said she immediately considered it "a pretext for our eviction." Betsy Fagin, a founder of the People's Library, said that many held the same suspicion: "We knew, because we co-ordinate with all the other occupations. Austin had been shut down that same day with exactly the same letter. So we knew that they were going to try to come and kick us out."

As soon as the notice hit the park, frenzied discussions arose among the occupiers as to how they should respond. An impromptu "People's Meeting"—a consensus-based meeting similar to the General Assembly, but lacking the latter body's formal organization or facilitators—was formed, and after passionate debate a consensus arose around one simple strategy. If the owners were concerned that Zuccotti was dirty, the occupiers would clean the park themselves.

But what did that entail? According to Andrew, a member of the Sanitation working group, a first priority was moving and "condensing" the personal belongings of occupiers. But such an effort proved tricky. Where would the belongings be moved—to storage? Would occupiers remove them from the park themselves? Furthermore, would all occupiers even heed the call to clean the park, or would some resist? By noon, Andrew said, early concerns were allayed as Zuccotti residents rose to the task—requests poured in to Sanitation for clear plastic bags, 50 brooms, two dozen mops. The demands of the clean-up effort quickly surpassed the supplies of the working group, which had only a single garbage-can-full of perhaps one dozen brooms.

While these requests streamed in, other occupiers set about informing and rallying Occupy movement supporters both inside the park and beyond. Within Zuccotti, as word spread of the occupiers' decision to clean the park themselves, enthusiasm mixed with a general sense of fear that eviction might be near. As the afternoon wore on, Sanitation managed to secure enough brooms and mops to fill the requests it had received and the occupiers formed what Andrew called a "Sanitation Army." The cleaning army continued packing up belongings and, by evening, began sweeping the park through and through, brushing the park's granite walks in successive waves.

Meanwhile, several working groups began reaching out to the movement's supporters in the New York community in preparation for the confrontation that they expected would come the next morning. Calls went out over the Internet, urging anyone who was able to make their way down to the park to help with the immense cleaning effort. The Labor Outreach Committee procured a strong showing of solidarity from New York City unions, contacting park employees, sanitation workers, and custodians particularly to help with the "clean up." Most significantly, many of the city's unions, including the Communications Workers of America, the United Auto Workers, and Service Employees International Union 1199 pledged to send members at 6 a.m. on the 14th—an hour before the scheduled cleaning— and the United Federation of Teachers also vowed to turn out members in solidarity. In an unprecedented move, the New York City-area AFL-CIO sent out an emergency email around 8 p.m. the night before the scheduled cleaning with the subject line reading "Go to Wall Street. NOW." Labor was also lending its support behind the scenes, according to Maida Rosenstein, president of UAW local 2110. "A lot of people were calling the mayor, and calling elected officials, and telling them to call the mayor," Rosenstein said. "People leveraging the clout they have with elected officials."

The legal working group was also quick to mobilize its network of support, urging "all available supporters" in individual community groups to come out at 6 a.m. The legal team conducted a comprehensive investigation of the claims made by Brookfield Properties in their notification letter. Armed with the results of that investigation and an upgraded official sanitation strategy coming from the Sanitation working group, the

National Lawyers Guild issued a notice of its own, directed to Brookfield Properties and Mayor Bloomberg, in which it denounced the proposed violation of First Amendment rights and warned that "prior court approval" would be required to carry out police action.

As community members, students and organized labor prepared to descend on Zuccotti early the following morning, the Sanitation Army continued apace through the night. Benjamin Shepard, an OWS activist, arrived at Zuccotti late in the evening, hoping to find some time to rest before the morning standoff. Upon arriving, however, Ben found the square packed with occupiers and allies. Many of those cleaning had already resigned themselves to a long night, including one older man, armed with a broom in one hand and a coffee cup in the other, who explicitly warned, "You guys are not going to get much sleep tonight. We're going to clean up all night, we need more coffee." The usually light-hearted spirit of the encampment was notably absent. It had also begun to rain. At first the drizzle was still light enough that, upon finding a sleeping spot shortly after midnight, Ben was able to spread a tarp and sheets and get some sleep. But just after 1 a.m. the drizzle intensified into a downpour, pelting his tarp and soaking his clothes through as it pooled and flowed along the park's granite surface. By 2 a.m., Ben had retired with some friends to the Blarney Stone, a nearby pub they had come to frequent.

Meanwhile, waves of broom-wielding protesters continued to sweep the length of the park, while others, including Amina Malika and her friend Mesiah painstakingly scrubbed the park surface on their hands and knees, repeatedly going back over spots that had already been rendered spotless several times before. If anything was less than sparkling, the occupiers feared that city authorities would use it to justify a cleaning of their own, not to mention an eviction. A driving, horizontal wind blew through the park, ensuring that everyone and everything was soaked through. While this was a nuisance for those attempting to sleep, the weather was on the side of those cleaning. Zuccotti Park is built on an incline, and the rain that poured into the park and blew sideways across its raised surfaces flowed down the length of the space and out, helping to sweep the park clean. As the rain poured and the thunder clapped Amina and Mesiah, giddy with exhaustion, cheered alongside their fellow cleaners—some of whom tore off their shirts in celebratory defiance of the storm.

Meanwhile, at the People's Library, the mood was less celebratory than frenetic. Earlier in the day, the librarians had moved half of the library's 5,000 or so books to a nearby storage space donated by the United Federation of Teachers. They had placed the other half of the library's holdings into plastic bins, wrapped in tarp against the expected rain, which were left on park benches so that the cleaning crews could sweep underneath. "We were just going to leave [the rest of the library] there and say, hey, this is important, it's part of the occupation, it stays," recalled Jaime, a People's Librarian. But at 2 a.m., as cleaning proceeded in the park and the rain intensified, plans changed abruptly. Jaime had managed only a couple of hours of sleep when her phone awoke her. "I get these panicky text messages from a couple of the librarians being like 'Oh my god, Sanitation tells us we have to move the library now! It has to go!'" Jaime recalled. "And the rest of us at home were like, 'Where's it going to go? Storage has been closed for five hours. We can't put it there. What are you even talking about?'" Those librarians in the park made a snap decision—the books would go to New Jersey. One protester had a friend with a place there. Another had a car. And so, in the frenzy of cleaning Zuccotti, half the contents of the People's Library were carted across the Hudson.

Just before 4 a.m., the rain abated and the cleaning effort slowed. Movement supporters began to flow into the park, the first of several waves that would ultimately swell the park's population to around 3,000. As throngs of people packed Zuccotti, keeping the park clean and tidy became the challenge. Any imperfection in the park's appearance, the occupiers feared, might prove enough of an excuse for Brookfield and Bloomberg. A major concern was the flowerbeds scattered throughout the park and ensuring they were not trampled. Calls to "watch the flowers!" rang out as some attempted to detour around the crowds by going through the flowerbeds. One photojournalist attempted such a maneuver only to find protester Kat Mahaney with her hand over his lens—she refused to give him a clear shot until he stopped crushing the flowers. Ted Hall, one of the Occupy camp's most visible members, stood atop the edge of a planter in the park's center, using the people's microphone to encourage those gathered. One occupier, KV, reported a sense of "electricity in the air" as the crowd amassed. The excitement grew as a contingent of hundreds descended on the park all at once—"The unions are here to back us up! THE UNIONS ARE HERE TO BACK U.S. UP!" someone shouted through the people's microphone to thunderous cheers. By 5 a.m. a group near Broadway had begun chanting, "Whose streets? Our streets!" and occupiers soon began waking up all who had been sleeping, giving them just under two hours to prepare for the expected confrontation. Tensions mounted, ratcheting with every "Mic Check! MIC CHECK!"

Shortly after 6 a.m., the hour at which occupiers had called on supporters to assemble, yet another "Mic Check!" was called by a woman perched on one of the marble walls at the park's edge. She informed those gathered, using their voices as amplification, that a plan was in place for holding the square, and that those who were not part of that plan—those who did not have a place and row assigned for them to sit and disobey a potential police order to move—were welcome to stay, but faced a high risk of arrest. Those in the crowd, she added, who could not be arrested were invited to cross the street and offer their support from sidewalks facing the park. "Waves of people repeated the invitation from the direct action working group to join them in linking arms and keeping the Plaza," recalled Marina Sitrin. "The response was resounding applause. There was no discussion, debate or hesitation. Not only did people agree with shouts, whistles, and their fingers twinkling in the air, but with their bodies." The sporadic flashes of press photographers twinkled as light began to creep into the sky.

Then, after 6:30 a.m. and just minutes shy of the cleaning deadline, another mic check rang out: "Mic check! MIC CHECK! I'd like to read a brief statement! I'D LIKE TO READ A BRIEF STATEMENT! From Deputy Mayor Holloway! FROM DEPUTY MAYOR HOLLOWAY! We received notice from the owners of Zuccotti Park! WE RECEIEVED NOTICE FROM THE OWNERS OF ZUCCOTTI PARK! Brookfield Properties that they are postponing their cleaning!" At which point the human mic fell to shouts of joy, which echoed through the crowd of thousands gathered, spreading the news without spreading the words—the Occupation had been saved. An explosion of screaming, laughter, embraces, and jubilant drumming erupted across the park. Smartphone screens lit up as many in the square began posting the news to their Twitter and Facebook feeds, and a marching band began to play near the *Joie de Vivre* sculpture in the park's southeastern corner. Chants quickly spread through the crowd: "We are the 99 percent!" and "We can change the course of history!" they echoed along with the human mic, which was now five waves deep. "We can defend this square from oppression!"

* * *

Once it was clear that the park was safe, calls for further action began to relay through the crowd via the people's microphone. Two marches were being considered: one to Wall Street, with the intention of finally occupying the financial district itself, and the other to City Hall, to thank Mayor Bloomberg for having halted the eviction proceedings, not to mention to "Show him what democracy looks like!" In a matter of minutes the crowd began pressing toward the northeastern corner of Zuccotti and, around the metal police barricades that still lined the sidewalks surrounding the park, the columns for both marches began to form. Protesters danced and chanted "We are the 99 percent!" as they spilled out onto the sidewalk along Broadway, accompanied by the steady pulse of the drummers who had come to symbolize the heart of the occupation. Staving off eviction had imbued the crowd with a renewed sense of power and confidence. Now, as at no time before during the Occupy Wall Street movement's nearly month-long presence in Lower Manhattan, it seemed possible to successfully stage a march on the heart of Wall Street. One contingent of marchers began moving south on Broadway toward Wall Street, many wielding the brooms they had used to clean Zuccotti hours earlier. The march carried with it the celebratory mood that had overtaken the park, and its spontaneity seemed to catch the NYPD off guard.

At first, police struggled to keep protesters on the sidewalks, an inability to manage the situation that was only punctuated by the question that chanters posed to any who would hear: "Whose streets?" along with its corresponding, booming response, "OUR STREETS!" Soon enough, however, a line of police scooters formed a V shape behind a segment of the march in an attempt to push protesters from the street. Toward the rear of the march most occupiers peacefully resisted the police, while at the head the rhythm of the Occupiers' drums reverberated as marchers leapt over police barriers to try to gain access to the streets adjacent to the New York Stock Exchange. Police met this advancing front of protesters with force, arresting several protesters and injuring several more. Others kept marching, snaking through the streets of lower Manhattan, chased all the way by police, whose sirens filled the streets. Confusion abounded as the march fragmented with every confrontation with the police. Phone calls and text messages, exchanged by friends who found themselves separated in the tumult, painted a chaotic scene—conflict near Bowling Green, wrong turns, arrests near Exchange Place.

As the march moved westward toward South Street Seaport, white-shirted senior-rank police officers pulled out batons to corral the march. By the time the group looped eastward on Maiden Lane and Pearl Street, the crowd started to run up the street, where the police had pushed activists into the street before arresting one young woman. "Its really hot out here," remarked a man with drums in his hands as the rallies overlapped. "We've been on cars drumming. It's a real riot out here." Several were arrested as the march continued to weave through the streets, and reports of excessive police force abounded—one man's leg was run over by a policeman on a scooter, VOCAL-NY leader Felix Rivera-Pitre was punched in the face by an officer. Ultimately the march retreated back to Zuccotti, after one marcher screamed, "Get back to the square! They are taking the square!"

Fears that police would take Zuccotti also plagued the second march, which headed north from the park toward City Hall. That march was less confrontational than the march on Wall Street, with protesters mostly sticking to the sidewalks and following the route marked by the police, who lined the edges of Broadway to prevent marchers from crossing into the street. Chants of "We are the 99 percent!" rang out, interspersed with the call-and-response, "Show me what democracy looks like! This is what democracy looks like!" and, "How do we fix this deficit? Stop the war! Tax the rich!" The celebratory mood was tempered as marchers approached the gates to City Hall Park, where vans of riot-geared officers awaited. Those officers, however, were assigned to preventing the march from entering the

City Hall complex, and when no one attempted to enter, the police merely stood by as the march continued to flow past. The march's stay at City Hall was short-lived, as word spread that Zuccotti was being taken by the police in the marchers' absence. Rattled, marchers began moving back down Broadway at a brisk pace, trying to balance the desire to get back to the park quickly with the need to maintain cohesion. As he walked back, Alex Gomez-del-Moral, one of the many who had arrived at Zuccotti Park between 5 and 6 a.m. was in the midst of a phone interview with a Toronto-based radio station, narrating the progress of the march. When the returning column of protesters burst back into the area around Liberty Plaza, he, like many around him, breathed a sigh of relief, and then reported what he had found: The only people in Zuccotti were the occupiers, soggy and weary but invigorated by the success of their all-night defense of the park.

As the morning wore on and those who marched to City Hall and Wall Street returned, a sense of exhausted normalcy settled across the park. Some went off in search of much-needed coffee or breakfast. Others attempted to sleep. Still others struck up discussions, and soon the sound of conversations and a steady drum beat once again filled the damp morning air of Zuccotti Park.

POCcupy—People of Color Occupy Wall Street Too!

"The POC's purpose is to keep the movement accountable, to keep these progressive white activists accountable, to have them understand that just because they are now feeling the pinch and the burn . . . it doesn't mean that peoples' worlds haven't been in turmoil for decades, for centuries."
—Jodi, member of the People of Color (POC) Working Group

The movement was beautiful. It was dusk and the lights, laid in the floor amongst the marble paving stones, flickered as the crowds ebbed and flowed above them, blocking their luminescence. A lone black woman in a black dress walked cautiously down the stairs on September 23, her first day at Zuccotti Park, and surveyed the scene. She looked left and right, and up at the "big Red Thing," and seemed interested in the conversations around her. But not recognizing anyone personally or by association, she waited awkwardly and in silence until the General Assembly started. She was lost in the crowd.

Jamie, a member of the People Of Color (POC) Working Group who describes herself as "the 99% and a person of color," first went down to Occupy Wall Street on October 15's National Day of Action. "I went by myself," she explained, "because no one else wanted to go with me. None of my friends were interested and I was just like, 'Well fuck it, I'm going to go check it out' . . . I loved the energy of it all . . . But what some people started to notice was that the GA was majority white and male, which is highest privilege you can have in this social construct that is our society. There are a lot of people who are of the 99% who look at these issues, issues that are most pertinent to them; issues that directly affect them every single day but they're not there [at Zuccotti Park] because they feel alienated, or they feel their voices won't be heard, or they've experienced racism."

Jodi, who first began going to Zuccotti Park on September 17, the first day of the Occupation, was able to witness the evolution of this initial lack of representation. "For the first week and a half I would come down a few times a week, and for the first two weeks there was not a presence of people of color," she said. "It was upsetting. Then at a certain point there was a burst or explosion and really a much more noticeable presence of people of color facilitating. I think it would have been ridiculous if it had continued on without more POC while presenting itself as a movement that represents the 'so-called 99 percent.'" Her sentiments have been repeated by many Occupiers, protesters, organizers, community activists and media outlets, all of whom who are still calling for a stronger presence of people of color and marginalized communities within the movement.

So on October 1, as tensions surrounding this feeling of alienation built, one woman stood up at the General Assembly and proposed a People Of Color Working Group, asking asked anyone interested to "Meet me at the Red Thing . . . now." Though she had discussed the idea with with many white allies and people of color, this earliest member of the POC group had nevertheless had to fend off two white men in order to get the proposal on the agenda in the first place. "Occupy Wall Street wasn't the diverse, safe space it professed to be," she later said. "I didn't expect it to be; the movement was created in a racially hostile society by individuals who bought into the dangerously flawed logic of colorblindness."

About five people, both people of color and white people, showed up to the initial meeting and exchanged emails. By the next meeting, the group attracted about 20 members—and by its third meeting about 100 people of all colors sat in a circle beneath the Red Thing and, through consensus, became a closed safe space for any person who identified as a person of color. Launched on October 1, 2011, the Call to People of Color from the OWS POC Working Group—the group's first document passed through consensus—read as follows:

> *To those who want to support the Occupation of Wall Street, who want to struggle for a more just and equitable society, but who feel excluded from the campaign, this is a message for you. To those who do not feel as though their voices are being heard, who have felt unable or uncomfortable participating in the campaign, or who feel as though they have been silenced, this is a message for you. To those who haven't thought about Occupy Wall Street but know that radical social change is needed, and to those who have thought about joining the protest but do not know where or how to begin, this is a message for you. You are not alone. The individuals who make up the People of Color Working Group have come together because we share precisely these feelings and believe that the opportunity for consciousness-raising presented by #OccupyWallStreet is one that cannot be missed. It is time to push for the expansion and diversification of #OccupyWallStreet. If this is truly to be a movement of the 99%, it will need the rest of the city and the rest of the country.*
>
> *Let's be real. The economic crisis did not begin with the collapse of the Lehman Brothers in 2008. Indeed, people of color and poor people have been in a state of crisis since the founding of this country, and for indigenous communities, since before the founding of the nation. We have long known*

that capitalism serves only the interests of a tiny, mostly white, minority.

Black and brown folks have long known that whenever economic troubles 'necessitate' austerity measures and the people are asked to tighten their belts, we are the first to lose our jobs, our children's schools are the first to lose funding, and our bodies are the first to be brutalized and caged. Only we can speak this truth to power. We must not miss the chance to put the needs of people of color–upon whose backs this country was built–at the forefront of this struggle.

The People of Color Working Group was formed to build a racially conscious and inclusive movement. We are reaching out to communities of color, including immigrant, undocumented, and low-wage workers, prisoners, LGTBQ people of color, marginalized religious communities such as Muslims, and indigenous peoples, for whom this occupation ironically comes on top of another one and therefore must be decolonized. We know that many individuals have responsibilities that do not allow them to participate in the occupation and that the heavy police presence at Liberty Park undoubtedly deters many. We know because we are some of these individuals. But this movement is not confined to Liberty Park: with your help, the movement will be made accessible to all.

If it is not made so, it will not succeed. By ignoring the dynamics of power and privilege, this monumental social movement risks replicating the very structures of injustice it seeks to eliminate. And so we are actively working to unite the diverse voices of all communities, in order to understand exactly what is at stake, and to demand that a movement to end economic injustice must have at its core an honest struggle to end racism.

The People of Color working group is not meant to divide, but to unite, all peoples. Our hope is that we, the 99%, can move forward together, with a critical understanding of how the greed, corruption, and inequality inherent to capitalism threatens the lives of all peoples and the Earth.

As Razzle, one of its members, explained, "The People Of Color Working Group was founded to help unify, through this one movement, the diverse communities that have been affected by economic inequality in different ways, with full awareness that this process of unification would require what had been missing from the Occupy Movement: greater participation, perspective and leadership of people of color with an explicit commitment to racial justice." Jodi similarly described that, "POC's purpose is to keep the movement accountable, to keep these progressive white activists accountable, to have them understand that just because they are *now* feeling the pinch and the burn . . . it doesn't mean that peoples' worlds haven't been in turmoil for decades, for centuries." According to Jamie, "one of the main objectives of POC is to have people of color represented in every single Working Group, particularly in the GA and within the leaders and the people who make the decisions . . . the POC Working Group *had* to be established as a protective measure and a way to represent the real issues at stake."

POC felt that the best way to accomplish these goals was to establish itself as a caucus within OWS, one which they hoped could expand to include all marginalized voices. They envisioned the role of such a caucus as not just to "provide a supportive and empowering space for people of color in the movement, but also to bring people of color and a racial justice lens to the leadership of this movement." For them, the practical purpose of having a caucus was to give the group the ability to work closely with *each* working group, as opposed to having POC confined to just one. As such, though the POC Working Group continues to meet as a separate entity, its caucus structure allows it to maintain subcommittees affiliated with an assortment of other OWS groups. These include Outreach, Education, Press,

Arts and Culture, Facilitation, Language Access, Immigrant rights, Safer Spaces, Child Care, Prison Solidarity, Police Brutality, Labor, Student Liaison, Finance, and Internet, among others. The POC subcommittees are empowered through the caucus to represent POC in the larger OWS working groups and to organize and host events, teach-ins, and direct actions. This caucus structure has remained in place with the implementation of the Spokes Council through the NYC GA.

Meanwhile, groups like Occupy the Hood, which had similar goals, emerged and began to work with the POC—a boon for the movement because increasing POC presence has made marginalized groups feel more comfortable becoming involved with OWS and attending GAs across the city. Yet, despite this, some of the concerns raised early in the movement around issues of race continue to be a deterrent for people of color who have not participated directly within OWS and even people of color within OWS have continued to experience incidences of explicit racism and racial micro-aggressions.

On Columbus Day (referred to as Indigenous Peoples' Day by POC), *Mexica*, an indigenous, cultural Mexican performance group began to dance in the space under the Red Thing. Moving to the beat of the drums, dancers dressed in white and red, becoming the beat themselves, as the beaded bracelets on their ankles entranced a crowd of about 100 people. The group was performing a number of sacred ceremonies and dances, each meant to honor Mother Earth and their ancestors and to send energy out to all the buildings surrounding the park. They thus hoped to push people towards justice and peace. But despite their efforts, POC members overheard those in the crowd making snide, oppressive remarks about the ceremony.

This was not an isolated occurrence. Since its beginnings, POC meeting attendees had been airing grievances ranging from small, privilege-related altercations to full-blown racist attacks and sexual assaults. And the grievances reported were not just limited to what had happened in Manhattan. On October 8, members of Occupy Philadelphia reached out to the OWS POC caucus for help regarding what they called "A Black Out at Occupy Philadelphia," where black women had been called racial slurs and then forced to leave the camp. Later in the month, members of Occupy Boston contacted the POC caucus for help integrating racially separate General Assemblies in their city. And when a General Assembly started in Brooklyn, the POC caucus was there to point out that organizers had failed to reach out to the majority of their community (people of color) when calling for their meeting and choosing its space. As conversations about police brutality got heated before and after the eviction, the POC caucus, through its prison solidarity subcommittee, hosted several teach-ins about the prison industrial complex and police brutality, sharing and discussing with the larger OWS movement how people of color and immigrant communities have been and are consistently policed and brutalized by the state. Some involved in the POC caucus raised an important yet, in their opinion, invisible issue about who can afford to get arrested and who can't, bringing up the fact that people of color, particularly men of color, are already targeted by the prison system and police.

More recently, POC members felt disrespected and silenced at Spokes Council meetings in early November when they stood up for one another in what they perceived to be the face of privilege, ignorance and racism. These tensions and problems reflect existing power structures and layers of oppression in the larger world. While OWS is working to create a different world, the Spokes Council is meant to be a movement towards a more just and equitable world. But many involved in both the POC caucus and the Spokes Council have expressed serious concerns, arguing that the council operates with little accountability and space to express grievances with the process. As such, a number of people in POC are currently working to challenge and transform the Spokes Council. At least two oppression workshops and racial justice trainings are being organized for late November, and the POC caucus has proposed that they be targeted specifically to Spokes Council participants.

As these tensions highlight, the POC Working Group has been in constant discussion over its "place" in the movement, its relationships with white allies, and its participation in direct actions. This has unearthed the many differences within the group as women and members of the LGBTQ community have, at times, felt excluded and disrespected. People of color from different socioeconomic, educational, and religious backgrounds also started to feel excluded. In such a large and diverse community, the moniker "People Of Color" encompasses a great deal of difference as privilege works on many levels including, but not limited to, race, class, gender, religion, and sexual norms. This can divide any group, even with common interests and goals.

Moving forward, the POC caucus feels it must deal with internal divisions by finding points of commonality between each of the diverse groups that has been marginalized by a patriarchal white supremacist society. Some argue that only allowing access to those who identify as "people of color" is exclusive and divisive within itself, but the majority of the group desires a space where people from already marginalized communities can convene without feeling oppressed, uncomfortable around, or hindered by those with privileges that they do not hold. As the POC caucus understands very well, systems of domination are most often perpetuated unknowingly by members of dominant groups and are most often played out through notions of entitlement and invisible privilege. The group thus participates in weekly conversations about how to create such a space that is inclusive while also guaranteeing the mental, physical and spiritual safety of all. Building across a multitude of differences, POCcupy continues to work to bring people together, in a positive and strong-spirited community.

Though these debates continue, the POC caucus has begun a

concerted push for positive direct actions. In addition to establishing a safe space for dialogue, the POC caucus has planned teach-ins about oppression and racism, planned days of healing, supported The Council of Elders (a group of leaders from many of the defining American social justice movements of the 20th century), and organized racial justice trainings both for the group itself and for the entire OWS movement. The POC caucus has also endorsed direct actions sponsored by those communities of color engaging in economic and social justice work, including Occupy the Hood, Occupy 477, Movement for Justice in El Barrio, and the Audre Lorde Project.

Of these, one of the most publicized events was an action the POC undertook in conjunction with Occupy 477 in Harlem. On November 6, 2011, at a regularly scheduled POC Working Group meeting, Semi, an organizer supporting occupy movements around the country brought a proposal to the POC Working Group urging it to support Occupy 477 in Harlem. This group was initially organized to preserve a historical landmark and low-income residential building located at 477 West 142nd Street in the Sugar Hill district of Harlem. Though the building had lofty origins—Alexander Hamilton had once lived there—it had been without heat and hot water wince October 2010 when, in a predatory lending scheme, law firms Madison Park Investors LLC and E.R. Holdings LLC attempted to foreclose on the property. In the process, they hoped to subvert the co-owners association, flip the building, and, ultimately, gentrify the neighborhood. Tenants were caught in the crossfire; the firms' method of driving out the building's residents was to turn off the heat. The companies also sabotaged the boiler and repeatedly prevented city workers from entering the boiler room to inspect it or make repairs.

In a time when there is a nationwide effort to stop foreclosures and an approaching winter season, news of the tenants' ordeal was a shocking reminder of the increasingly violent tactics used to gentrify Harlem and drive out residents who had lived there since the late 1970s. POC members, particularly those from Occupy The Hood, were determined to bring a proposal in front of the GA and have OWS help Occupy 477 reclaim the building and make it livable; POC members empowered an ad hoc group of the POC Caucus to draft an emergency proposal asking the GA for emergency supplies and funding for the building's occupiers. Some short time later, 15 members of the POC marched over to the GA, already in session, and brought the emergency proposal to the crowd. (run on)

As with most proposals, there were some points of contentions, questions, and concerns; the POC members at the GA worked hard to respond to questions and accept friendly amendments, one of which was to in fact ask for more funds. Many of the concerns raised at the GA had to do with why this proposal constituted an emergency, and POC members had to remind the crowd that the people of Occupy 477 were fighting for their housing rights, fighting for their own building, and doing so against the unjust economic structures OWS was founded to counter.

Ultimately, the GA reached consensus on the proposal to support Occupy 477 with $3,000 for supplies, help with the boiler, and assistance for occupiers defending the building. A great sense of empowerment and amazement washed over members of the POC at the GA that evening–some who felt, for once, they finally had a real voice within the OWS movement. Today, occupiers are still at Occupy 477, providing inspiration for members of the Harlem community and people of color struggling with the right to shelter. And Occupy 477 has shown a supportive and consistent presence at Liberty Park, hosting teach-ins and marches, as well as Occupy 477's Queen Mother being on the Council of Elders.

As the movement's momentum builds and as it gains support from those already active in social and economic justice, people in the POC caucus remain committed to its ideal of complete representation and participation of communities of color. Many in the POC caucus and the larger OWS reflect upon the words of Angela Davis, who spoke to protesters on October 30 at the Washington Square Park General Assembly and argued for the necessity of diverse representation within the movement. Davis said:

> All minorities are the majority . . . We have to learn how to be together in a complex unity, in a unity that does not leave out our differences, in a unity that allows those whose voices have been historically marginalized to speak out on behalf of the entire community. I am sure as the days and months go by, we will all learn more about this process than we now know. It is important that this movement expresses the will of the majority from the outset, but that majority must be respected in terms of all the differences within.

Following Davis' lead, the POC works to ensure equitable involvement of all marginalized groups, and a racial justice lens that also takes into account other aspects of identities (such as gender, class, sexuality, religion, language, nationality, and ability.) It is upon achieving these goals, as its members continually and stridently remind us, that OWS will gain the power it needs to create a more just world.

AUTHORS' STATEMENT: Three active members of the POC caucus engaged in the collective writing of this descriptive piece meant to offer a narrative history of the POC within the OWS movement. We want to assert our voices here and let readers know that this is only but a fraction of the stories and voices of POC in the movement. There are many voices not included here, which were and continue to be instrumental in the building of POCcupy and the OWS movement. We want to acknowledge all the voices not included and offer transparency in the creation of this document, which required an extreme turn around. Due to time constraints and publishing deadlines, we were not able to include more voices, and so we chose not to use a collective "we" in the writing of this piece. We were able to share only four of the interviews conducted with POC in OWS. The stories told here come from a combination of our experiences and first hand work within POCcupy.

At the Edge of the Square

*"I tried to sell good derivatives, I tried to sell
good derivatives, derivatives aren't inherently bad!"*
*—An investment banker making a late night visit to the
OWS Information Desk at the east end of Zuccotti Park*

Shortly after the October snow—which blanketed the encampment in an inch of slush—an elderly couple approached William Scott as he sat on the edge of the eastern sidewalk, near the People's Library. "I know everybody's thinking about the same thing, but I am so worried about you guys," the woman said in her thick Queens accent. "This winter: How are you going to survive it? How are you going to stay here with the storms, with the snow?" Scott replied, "We stayed here the other night with that Nor'easter." But his response did little to obviate her concern. "That's what I'm saying! That's not healthy for you guys!" The woman's husband then pulled a wad of cash out of his pocket and insisted on making a donation so that Scott and the other occupiers could buy "those silver things!" by which he meant space blankets.

* * *

After September of 2011, as occupiers settled on Zuccotti's granite walkways, the park came to be cordoned from the smooth ebb and flow of daily foot traffic. The NYPD lined the park's surrounding streets with portable metal fencing, open only at street intersections, effectively using the park's surrounding sidewalks as buffer zones between what had become Liberty Plaza and the police lines. Over the course of the two-month encampment, as Zuccotti blossomed into a full-fledged micro-city, these sidewalk no-man's-lands came to serve as vibrant zones of contact, where occupiers and opportunists intermingled with casual visitors as well as with the police.

Far from a homogenous buffer, the four sidewalks that make up Zuccotti's perimeter quickly took the form of distinct zones, each with different sorts of interactions, shaped by particularities in the internal organization of the occupation itself.

The sidewalk along Cedar Street, on the park's southern edge and abutting the sleeping area, was relatively quiet, the interactions there, for the most part, muted in tone and commercial in nature. The south side saw a much lighter police presence than did the park's other sidewalks, and, but for the occasional news crew which sometimes parked their vans along Cedar, tended to be sparsely populated by a few halal food and coffee carts near Broadway and a sporadic souvenir vendor here and there (yes, they capitalized on OWS too). One airbrush artist set up a makeshift T-shirt business on the park's south side, in one instance customizing a shirt that read "Occu-Princess" for a little girl visiting the encampment with her mother.

Depending on the time of day, or constantly in the early weeks of the occupation, the closer one got to Trinity Place, walking along the park's southern sidewalk, the louder became the PULSE—the occupy drummers, who had claimed the steps on the park's west side. The drummers' location, combined with the Tree of Life and community altar (piled high with candles, beads, plants, fruit and burning sage incense) near Zuccotti's northwest corner, gave the park's western edge a more spiritual vibe. But that didn't stop the occasional dance party from breaking out. One evening in early October, a group of bicyclists from Times Up! (a New York-based environmental group advocating direct action) descended on the park's western edge with a special "sound bike"—pumping Jay-Z, New Order, James Brown and Public Enemy tunes as occupiers danced, let off a little steam and chanted, "All day! All week! Occupy the beats!" Brennan Cavanaugh, an OWS activist who helped organize the impromptu dance party, recalled, "This was before they had all the barricades up around the park, and you could come and go easily. There were still no walls, and people just started running out, and running along side us pumping their fists in the air!" Eventually, police pushed the dancers down the block, and within a matter of days the barricades along Trinity were set.

The drummers and sacred space made the park's western sidewalk highly popular among tourists, who could often be seen snapping photos or stopping to chat with the hare krishnas in their white robes. This tourist presence usually brought a handful of sign-holders to the park's western edge—protesters, some from within the park, some visiting in solidarity, who left their mark on the occupation with pithy appeals scrawled on just about anything. Pizza boxes were a particularly common material. At first this was just because there were so many of them around, but as the pizza box sign attained an iconic status within the movement, Amy Roberts, a part-time public librarian and an OWS archivist explained, visitors looking to leave their personal stamp on Zuccotti began to "make a point of doing it on the pizza boxes." Said Roberts, who collected many of the signs left behind by visitors to the park."They're all hand-made, not sort of pre-packaged . . . It's actually interesting because some of the signs I've seen I haven't heard people say, but I wish they would. But maybe that's the way they express their voice, is in making a sign. So, to me it's like a really big part of how the movement expresses itself."

The number of sign-holders increased as one turned the corner onto Zuccotti's northern sidewalk. Liberty Street, the park's northern boundary, featured a most dramatic staging of police presence that included dozens of officers and a wide-array of NYPD vehicles at all times, a show of force that often completely closed the street to through-traffic. By mid-October, police had erected a portable surveillance tower, which some in the Class War Camp, a makeshift anarchist info shop in the park's western interior, dis-affectionately called the "Star Wars tower." Along the park's northern sidewalk, many occupiers responded to the pseudo-militarized space on the other side of the barricades with an almost quotidian protest idiom. Pedestrians attempting to scurry past Zuccotti along this sidewalk would spy occupying buskers, who often sat along the northern sidewalk playing folk tunes on guitar and collecting money for laundry. One chilly October late afternoon, a grandmother sat with a similarly gray-haired friend knitting hats, scarves and mitts for the occupiers, all while facing a line of New York's Finest who killed time waiting for their shift along the barricades to end. Among other things, the grandmother's sign included a list of "wants": "End the war(s) _ Abolish the Death Penalty _ Increased taxes on the wealthiest (tax equity) _ A better America for my grand kids please."

As the weather began to cool in late October, and the police and fire departments began confiscating gasoline-powered generators, the park's northern sidewalk came to feature a row of stationary bikes, which visitors and occupiers alike took turns riding in order to power manual generators. This frequently brought a crowd of onlookers, who mingled in conversation with fellow onlookers and occupiers alike. While most sign-holders along the park's northern sidewalk angled for photographers, many also actively engaged in these conversations. One regular, a 20-something Brooklyn resident named Jose, who sported a mustache-goatee combo, his Marine dog tags and a cardboard sign proclaiming "END THE FED," was one sign holder who actively sought conversation with passers-by. "I've been talking about End The Fed here ever since this started on the 17th," said Jose one evening in early October. "I figure why sit around and watch movies, this is the place to be right now."

While sign-holders and conversations were certainly present on the park's western and northern sidewalks, they became especially concentrated on the park's northeastern corner. A raised planter along the park's northern sidewalk approaching Broadway, in particular, became a focal point for sign-holders, who used the low marble wall as a perch from which to draw attention. One such sign holder, a man with tennis-ball yellow hair and a bright orange jacket, sat on the wall one October evening with a sign reading, "Yet Another Green Haired Deer Hunting Real Estate Redeveloper in Support of OWS." Others taped signs to the wall—signs bearing slogans such as "Shut Down Indian Point," "For A Nuclear Free Carbon Free Future," "Radical Joy For Hard Times [featuring a line drawing of a swallow swooping toward a jagged nest]." Also taped to the wall one could at times find political cartoons, as well as signs perhaps taped in lieu of the vigorous debates they might otherwise provoke—like one promoting a "First in the Nation Caucus Occupation," during the Iowa Caucuses in January, and others by a conspiracy theorist called Jeff Boss, who believed the National Security Administration was involved in the 9/11 terrorist attacks and claimed that the OWS camp's food had been tainted with a slow-acting poison.

The corner, which attracted many tourists and photographers, also served as a space for the public reclaiming of symbols. In addition to several waving American flags, Stephen, a Latino student of politics and business at LaGuardia Community College, waved a yellow Gadsden Flag—the yellow flag, bearing a rattlesnake and the phrase "Don't Tread On Me," which had of late become synonymous with the Tea Party movement. Speaking in a hoarse voice, which suggested he had been defending his choice of flag for hours, even days, Stephen said, "The reason I came with this flag is because this is the first flag our country united under to fight against imperialism, so this is very significant to me. Not only that, but the Tea Party movement, corporate elite, the captains of industry, international bankers, all these people have hijacked our government, hijacked our country and hijacked America and we're taking it back! This doesn't belong to the Tea Party! They have not been tread on; they don't care about their country, they care about their bank accounts!"

Stephen spoke in a fast, indefatigable cadence, making it difficult to get a word in edge-wise. Such a pattern of speech was not uncommon among the regulars of the park's eastern sidewalk, which became an epicenter of fevered conversations and debates. The sidewalk, running alongside Broadway, sat elevated above the rest of Zuccotti park, which lay at the bottom of stairs at the sidewalk's edge—creating a backdrop effect that displayed the whole eastern half of the park, making it photogenic and a space much utilized by journalists conducting interviews. Protesters and visitors clearly wishing to be interviewed, or at least to be engaged with, tended to amass on the park's eastern sidewalk, creating a teeming scene that served as a magnet for conservatives and bankers trying to better understand the occupiers, or perhaps to try their hand at proving them wrong. At times, such interactions became heated to the point of near violence. One mid-October evening a middle aged occupier, wearing all denim and sporting a red bandana around his neck, was roused to anger by a fellow middle-aged Long Islander who had used the phrase "you liberals" during their discussion—fighting words for the self-described socialist who tensed up in preparation for fisticuffs, before his unintentional instigator walked away, finding a fight not worth his time.

Daniel Levine, a 22-year-old student at Baruch College who often manned the OWS Information Desk on the eastern sidewalk, had a front-row seat for many of these altercations, verbal and otherwise. "Somebody punched this man in a skirt in the face," Levine recalled. "We had to call a mic check and form a human wall around him. We've had a couple of incidents like that in front of the table because we're right on the street so people—I guess people that want to instigate are too lazy to come into the square so they come over here." A self-proclaimed conversationalist and lover of stories, Levine would often man info desk east for as many as 18 hours at a stint. While the work suited Levine, the information desk could prove too intense for some—as it often meant exposing oneself to a highly concentrated dose of the heated interactions on the park's eastern edge. William Scott, an associate professor of English at the University of Pittsburg who dabbled in working at the info desk before joining the staff of the People's Library, said the work drove him nuts. "It's just this never-ending stream of people asking stuff. And about one in every five questions is a legitimate question that actually has something to do with us," Scott recalled. "The other four of the five are like, 'So what the hell are you guys doing down here anyway?'"

But if the eastern sidewalk attracted those with questions about and critiques of the occupation, it also served as a site of absolution. Levine recalled one late-night visit by investment bankers: "I guess they heard the drumming all day and it was this tell-tale-heart sort of thing and they just felt really guilty they were giving me this, 'I tried to sell good derivatives, I tried to sell good derivatives, derivatives aren't inherently bad!'" Levine said. "And then they gave like 20 bucks to the donation bin. It was very odd, it was like a confessional booth at night here the first couple of weeks."

After more than a month staffing the desk, Levine confessed that he rarely went into Liberty Plaza much anymore—his daily life as part of Occupy Wall Street, as he put it, revolved not around the kitchens, or the General Assembly, and certainly not around PULSE's drumming. His life, as he put it "revolves around this table."

Others based on the periphery still felt engaged with the rest of the Square. Patricia, a Chilean woman volunteering with the Información en Español working group, said her morning destination was also a desk—the working group's pamphlet-strewn table along the walkway at the south-eastern corner of the park, near the red statue—but she, unlike Levine, typically began her day by taking a walk around the park to get a feel for what was going on that day, always followed by a visit to the Info/Media booth just inside the square from the People's Library in the park's north-eastern quadrant.

The interactions along the park's sidewalks were always framed by the police presence. While cross-barricade conversations were common along the northern and eastern sidewalks, they mostly consisted of tourists requesting directions to the Century 21 department store a block to the north, or to Ground Zero, or to the nearest restroom. On occasion, however, the significance of the state power represented by the barricades—if not the actual metal fences themselves—seemed to temporarily recede. In late October, a handful of male police officers stood immersed in conversation among themselves on the Broadway side of the park's eastern barricade. Perhaps ten feet away stood a young white woman with a cardboard sign reading, "Clap twice if you're in debt." Upon registering her presence, a tall white officer, breaking the fourth wall of the barricade, shouted "Oh!" and clapped his hands twice, smiling. His fellow officers paused their conversation, looking at him in confusion. "It says clap if you're in debt," the cop explained to his fellow officers, matter-of-factly, "I'm in debt." Smiles broke out as the officers began to realize the "joke"—that they shared more in common with those across the barricade than with those had who ordered the streets barricaded. "I'm in debt too!" one chimed in. Another said, with a sense of light-hearted finality, "Everyone's in debt."

Washington Square, Times Square

"I am an immigrant. I came to take your job.
But you don't have one."
—On a sign held by Ilektra Mandragou, in Times Square

At five o'clock, on October 15, daylight had not yet faded, but Time Square's billboards and buildings were lit up. The square was on the edge of being more crowded than usual. A group of stilt-walkers and a brass band—some members of the Rude Mechanical Orchestra—congregated in the center of the square, bound by advertisements for Broadway's production of *Bonnie & Clyde* and the Bank of America building. Groups of OWS supporters—including students, Teamsters and UAW members— stood in small clusters, holding signs. Two dark-haired, bearded graduate students self-consciously, but insistently, thrust a hand-lettered sign in front of one of the news cameras that dotted the square. It read: "Cash Rules Everything Around Me. Destroy Capitalism." Some tourists gawked, then moved on. A couple from Pennsylvania asked if this was OWS and if anything was going to happen, if more people were coming or if the clumps of people standing idly, if expectantly, with signs was "it." "We're here to support OWS," shrugged the taller of the two bearded students, "but who knows how big this will get." He glanced at the metal barricades that were already in place, and again thrust his sign above his head.

By 6 p.m., Times Square was packed with Occupy Wall Street supporters, many of whom were, or would become, members of the emerging NYC All Student Assembly, a group formed in support of OWS and also intent on kicking off a student movement in its own right.

* * *

The first all-city student assembly in solidarity with Occupy Wall Street was held on Saturday, October 8, in Washington Square Park, a public space centrally located in Greenwich Village next to NYU's main campus.

Students were part of Occupy Wall Street from its beginnings, and the issue of student debt had been a prominent one. While never solely a youth movement, the voices of a generation determined not to passively accept an unjust order reverberated in every action. During one of the earliest marches on Wall Street, a George Washington University law student fell to his knees in the street and shouted out the story of his parents, both of whom held graduate degrees. As he spoke, he beckoned to a building façade nearby: "That's the bank that took my parents' home . . . They [my parents] played by the rules . . . I would rather die than be quiet and watch everything that they worked for go away . . . I'm not moving . . . I'm not going to be quiet." Shortly after, at his own request, the man was arrested.

In the weeks that followed, students and teachers in New York City area schools, public and private, secondary and collegiate, had begun to organize and coordinate action internally. There was, however, not much communication and cohesion between and among these groups, with much of the division along institutional lines. The all-city student assemblies, beginning on this October day and continuing each Saturday, sought to remedy this.

Facebook, a Google Groups site with an accompanying list-serv, fliers, and other media spread the word about the assemblies. The goal of the assemblies, as articulated by the facilitator (essentially a moderator) of the third weekly meeting, was to create, "a space for all the students of New York to come together and just figure out what we are as a movement, how we can become a movement, and how we can work together in our struggles." Drawing students, teachers, and graduates from schools within and without the city, representatives of student activist groups such as New York Students Rising, members of the OWS Empowerment and Education working group, graduate employee unions and even parents concerned with the debt they and their college-enrolled children were incurring, the assemblies became a forum for relevant announcements, the sharing of stories, and, most immediately, the coordination of action and community-building efforts. They began to plan for a Student Day of Action.

CUNY students who make up the majority of New York's student population were involved in organizing this day of action. Long subject to tuition hikes at public colleges that were once free, CUNY students were again facing expected $1,500 increase later in the fall. Meanwhile, CUNY Graduate students and adjunct professors worked with increasingly large class sizes, no raises and faced cuts to their already minimal health care coverage.

The CUNY Graduate Center became a major site for the initial stages of organizing the citywide student movement. Students, many of whom are also adjunct professors, were able to mobilize via networks forged as part of the PSC/CUNY's adjunct project. Students also held walkouts, teach-ins and meetings at Hunter College, Baruch, City College and Brooklyn College. At this stage, the organization spread even to Medgar Evers College, a campus where little recent student activism had taken place. Undergraduate organizers explicitly took inspiration from the storied CUNY student organization SLAM which took on tuition increases in the 1990s, as well as the 1969 occupation of City College by the black and Puerto Rican students, an action which resulted in the "open admissions policy" for CUNY and the effective desegregation of the CUNY system.

Nevertheless, the spread-out geography of the CUNY system, its size and the busy lives of working-class CUNY students who often balance school, work parenthood and other family obligations, make CUNY organizing a mammoth task. The planning for the Day of Action was greatly helped by an alliance with students in private colleges.

Before Occupy Wall Street, alliances between students at public and private colleges and universities across the city benefited from the unionization of student workers and more general union support. Many student activists in New York Students Rising were members of Communication Workers of America (CWA) graduate employee locals. They had been active in the March 4 Day of Action earlier that year against tuition hikes, departmental cuts and other attacks on Higher Education that a growing number of students understood to be connected to the nationwide attacks on collective bargaining and the U.S. working class. NYU students have also been involved in local union fights, lending support to adjunct faculty contract negotiations (the adjunct faculty at NYU and the New School are both represented by UAW Local 7902), the Teamsters art-handlers who are currently locked out of Sotheby's and Stella D'Oro workers. NYU graduate student workers themselves are still in the midst of a recognition campaign for their union, GSOC-UAW Local 2110.

Unionized graduate student employees kept abreast of union struggles across campuses and cities through their parent unions, but also other social justice networks, including the Coalition for Graduate Employee Unions (CGEU)—a loose affiliation of graduate employee unions and allies from the U.S. and Canada that holds a yearly conference. In August 2011, CGEU was held at New York University. It brought in speakers from Madison, Wisconsin, where their graduate union was active in the fight against Governor Scott Walker's anti-collective bargaining initiatives. Other speakers included law student activists from the University of Puerto Rico, who spoke of the global threat to public, accessible higher education and workers' rights—a threat that New York area students followed on Facebook and Twitter posts from activists in Greece, India, England, and across the world.

At NYU, students, faculty and staff had also been active in a nearly four-year-long campaign for the rights of migrant workers who build, operate and maintain non-U.S. site branch campuses, particularly NYU Abu Dhabi. NYU undergraduates also organized the Tuition Reform Action Committee (TRAC) and Students Creating Radical Change (SCRC) in the years leading up the occupation of the NYU Kimmel Student Center in February 2009. The NYU occupation took direct inspiration from the December 2008 student occupation of the New School. Organizers there were in contact with those in the University of California system, where student occupiers at the University of Santa Cruz famously issued no demands and issued a manifesto explaining why.

Such networks helped galvanize and firm up support between students and their affinity groups for mass NYC student action, which let to an all New York City student speak-out as part of the OWS National Day of Action that preceded the convergence at Times Square. The students could not have anticipated the events of the previous day—an attempted eviction foiled by a mass mobilization helped by labor, MoveOn and other supporters—but these, of course, boosted the energy and the numbers of the long-planned protest.

* * *

From the earliest days of the movement, personal story-telling had helped to build solidarity—and to put faces on OWS and better explain it to the outside world. For many, a desire to exorcise associated frustrations–toward positive ends, if possible–was deeply motivating. At general assemblies and the all-city student meetings, current and former students expressed anxiety and even despair at the prospect of continued debt accrual. For them, the stakes were high. The Occupy movement represented more to them than a pet social project or an experiment in radical grassroots politics: it offered a chance at redemption from what seemed to be impossible financial obligations.

The student speak-out in Washington Square Park, a public park at the heart of a private college campus, attracted as many as 600 participants at any one time. A facilitator took stack and one by one, students riffed on why they were participating in the day's action. The human mic doubled every story, sending it to the back of the crowd at the south end of the park. Many of the students present had mobilized the night before to block the attempted eviction from Zuccotti Park, yet instead of being exhausted, they were emboldened and they spoke with an urgent understanding of the need for solidarity.

One woman, a mother who decided to go back to school after a decade of raising children, spoke up about how much she loved her coursework, but also her fear that even with a degree in social work, she could never repay her student loans—much less afford tuition for her own near-college age children. An energetic young woman stood up to give an impromptu teach-in on student loans, their similarity to the mortgage crisis and the predatory practices of lenders. Several graduate students bemoaned recent cuts to graduate funding at the federal level. Another man, down from Vermont, mentioned joining the speak-out not because he is a student, but because he'd like to be. At twenty years old, unemployed and unable to afford school, he said, "my future seems bleak."

While debt and tuition were the main subjects of the day, one speaker, Jason Ide—a young college graduate and president of Teamsters Local 814—made an appeal for solidarity between students and workers like the locked-out members of his local who handle art for the city's elite auction houses. "We're in this together," he said. "Our members have gone without a paycheck for 12 weeks."

At the close of the speak-out, students broke into working groups, including a student of color working group, an anti-oppression and safe spaces group and an action group tasked with bottom-lining future happenings. They clustered around benches, pointing at the buttons they wore and holding up signs to show who they were and what brought them to Washington Square. A young man in a boy scout uniform with a bloody rubber foot protruding from an open khaki knapsack, walked from group to group, eventually following a cluster of students who set off to try and link back up with OWS proper. Other students split up to hold actions at local bank branches, which led to several arrests.

As the students dispersed, someone at the south end of the park yelled, "See you at the 5 o'clock dance!" And then began a slow convergence from all corners of the city into Times Square, where thousands of demonstrators—some students, many not— would gather, mingling with tourists and gawkers. Some came in a celebratory mood - after all, the movement had just defeated the mayor's attempt to shut down the camps in Zuccotti Park. Others felt the occupation was still vulnerable, and wanted to defend it. But all came, too, for the same reason people show up to every Occupy protest: to put an end to plutocracy.

Though police quickly made it impossible to easily traverse the square, leaving many demonstrators unable to join friends, family or affinity groups as planned, the demonstration still had a peaceful and high-spirited tone. The day coincided with ComicCon, a gathering of comic book fanatics from around the nation, and ZombieCon which is, according to its Web site, "a loosely organized group of bloodthirsty zombies" who "gather once a year to attack NYC in a theatrical, absurdist parody of blind consumerism and brainless politics." Attendees from both conventions joined the demonstrators in full character costume, lending the protest a unique visual flair, as superheroes and zombies mingled easily with the city's indignant, sign-wielding 99 percent.

Along with students, the imaginary and the undead, the Times Square protest drew families with children, workers, the jobless and young professionals. Ilektra Mandragou, a freelance designer, came with her husband, a CUNY graduate student and adjunct professor. She held a sign that said, "I am an immigrant. I came to take your job. But you don't have one." As more people joined the crowd, the news crawl over their heads read, "Occupy Wall Street Movement Goes Worldwide," a reference to the solidarity protests taking place in more than 80 countries that day.

The zombies, having started drinking at 1 p.m., went back downtown after about an hour, to continue their evening's revelry, which would endure until 4 a.m. But the ranks of the Times Square protesters continued to grow.

There were more than 80 arrests that day, which compared to the Brooklyn Bridge march, was not that many. But the heavy police presence was intimidating, and could be directed even toward the most harmless protesters. "My kids almost got arrested. We dove out right as the nets were coming down," says Rivka Little, a founder of 99 Percent School who has since become active in Occupy Harlem and Parents for Occupy Wall Street. "We had police mopeds aiming directly at us. It was scary." Her daughters—aged six and twelve—had spent most weekends at Zuccotti, throughout the occupation. While Rivka provided plenty of Fruit Roll-Ups and warm clothing to ease their participation, incidents like those at Times Square remind her kids that changing the world is serious business. As Rivka jokes all the time, "Is this a family outing or a revolution?"

For most families that day, however, the Times Square protest ended with nothing more dramatic than hunger. Under the Hard Rock Cafe sign, one five-year-old, adapting a conventional protest chant to his own ends, began heckling his parents, chanting, "The people! United! Will now have dinner!"

Not long after, a smaller crowd surged away from Times Square, back downtown toward Zuccotti Park, still, for the moment, the movement's hub, and still thriving.

The Art of the Square

*"We believe we are at the brink of a new art movement,
a new school of thought . . . hopefully you will join us . . ."*
—*Message from the OWS Arts and Culture
Sub-Committee to poets in the park*

Just as OWS seeks to redefine politics and democracy, so the arts component of the movement is interested in pushing the boundaries of what we consider art to be. The whole movement is about evolution and change, about shifting perceptions, about increasing our capacity for self-reflection. It is about giving people the tools to think clearly and critically about their place in their communities, global and local alike. In this respect participants in the arts groups believe their work serves just as vital a function as the GA. Whereas the GA makes decisions and builds community through conversation and cooperation, the artists' guilds seek to build consciousness, the fertile ground in which that community can flourish. "Before social practices change, and institutions change, you need to change the conversation," explained Alex Carvalho, a founding member of the Arts and Culture working group. "You need to change the aesthetics, you need to change the symbols, the images people use as a backdrop to frame the conversation in the first place."

These considerations about the movement's symbolism and representation have been a part of OWS since its inception. Arts and Culture formed in preparation for September 17, but also planned and participated in artistic actions throughout the summer. Alex in fact attributes "the first mass arrest of the movement" to Arts and Culture's failed attempt at occupying Wall Street on September 1. That night twelve members of the working group gathered with guitars, poems, and songs to protest the nation's economic crisis. Nine of the twelve were arrested after a confrontation with the police, who insisted that activists could not sleep on the cobblestoned street, but the action shows the participants' dedication to art as a form of political speech.

Their next action was more successful. On OWS's official first day, September 17, the group hosted the "New York Fun Exchange," a carnival on Bowling Green intended to critique New York's other famed exchange by engaging passersby through creative expression. Jez, one of the group's founders, explained that what he and his colleagues most wanted was to "make protests non-threatening, entirely peaceful, but symbolic and theatrical."

The group's planned schedule of events was thwarted when Jez arrived at Bowling Green to discover Wall Street barricaded. "I got there an hour or so in advance [of the carnival]," he explained, "and there were already people collected down there. A lot of people didn't really know what was going to happen. They were all hanging out and looking for stuff that they should be doing, not really knowing what to do." Arts and Culture's carefully printed flyers were meaningless with the intended space for actions blocked off. But though the confusion claimed some of the group's planned events, such as a folk singer who was not able to procure an amplification permit, the artists improvised.

"I tried to get people organized to have a parade around the bull," said Jez. It was surrounded by fences and "there were cops inside of the fences, and all I said was 'Let's make a parade'. . . .

We paraded a little conga line in which people were doing some chants and playing—I think I brought my bongos and so those were the only drums that we really had—but we just marched around the bull. Then I transitioned into trying to get people to do yoga." The day's events were many and varied, including teach-ins about economics, performances by roving choirs, and an "anti-capitalism evangelical preacher" named Reverend Billy. When Jez wasn't parading or doing yoga, he threaded through the crowd with fistfuls of flowers for those assembled. Looking back on that day, he opined about its significance: "We changed the nature of that space by stepping out there and calling attention to everybody that it was there, speaking to people and calling them to see themselves . . . as a group, as connected."

An ever more rich and varied community of artists emerged to explore this connection as the occupation took root. Zuccotti Park offered a rich, sensory stew as tents went up, walkways were delineated, and the park became a labyrinth of smoke, food smells, drums, instruments, information booths, meetings, bemused onlookers, and, of course, the heavy police presence. In this environment, Arts and Culture had a strategic approach to their art. Reg Flowers, a theater artist and community organizer from Brooklyn, put it aptly: "In the OWS movement, arts are not simply decoration or distraction, but rather tools to engage the base, send a clear message, and engage people who would not necessarily find a way in." No expression of artistic imagination was frivolous; it all served to lift protesters up or to help them fight back. Buttons with slogans encouraged passive spreading of the message; poster art flourished as people looked for ways to expand the occupation's "99%" brand to their neighborhoods and college campuses; the People's Stage was an open mic forum where people could express themselves without judgment.

Soon tourists and city residents began coming to Zuccotti simply to gawk at the spectacle; Joe Therrien was one of them.

He learned about the movement online, he said, and wanted to see for himself what it was about. Once at the park, he recalled, he "very quickly found out that there was this crazy spirit floating around Liberty Square, and just talking to people kind of blew my mind." Joe quickly became involved by founding the OWS Puppetry Guild and putting his MFA in the field to good use. At marches and rallies the Guild's creations are manned by multiple puppeteers who hold the figures aloft with the help of large poles. One, Lady Liberty, made one of her first appearances at Washington Square in early October, her eight-foot burlap body soaring above the crowd and lending a sense of gravitas to the proceedings. Every so often, puppeteers raised her arms skyward as if she were at once embracing and blessing the assembled multitudes. Others of the puppets were featured in Greenwich Village's annual Halloween Parade. The Puppetry Guild, in conjunction with the Arts and Culture working group, contributed banners and giant puppets to the march, along with one thousand OWS foot soldiers preaching the gospel of economic justice.

Another of the early artist groups was the Poetry Guild, which emerged in a similarly organic fashion. The first meeting of poets at Occupy Wall Street happened in late September when over 50 poets gathered for a poetry reading at Liberty Square. There was no headliner, no unifying style, no entrance fee, and–it's fair to say–no ordinary poetry reading. Their initial event, a weekly reading that came to be called the "Poetry Assembly," was organized and performed less like a poetry reading and more like a democratic Athenian assembly. Each voice was presumed to be equal and each had the prerogative to speak before the assembly. If the occupation was a horizontal and leaderless movement, poetry would be no different. Poets were chosen at random by lot and given no more than three minutes to read. Lines of poetry were repeated back to the poet using the same call-and-response method utilized regularly at Occupy Wall

Street. Writers present said they were not there simply there to demand for democracy, but to perform it.

Other events like this one soon led to calls for new artists' collectives to form at Occupy Wall Street. As an e-mail from the Arts and Culture Sub-Committee to the poets stated, "We believe we are at the brink of a new art movement, a new school of thought. To catalyze that, we are creating collectives inside our Arts and Culture to advance our movement and society aesthetically towards a new paradigm. We have already a collective on performance art, one is music, and hopefully you will join us with poetry." The poets joined, as did a multitude of others. Today the list of guilds affiliated with Arts and Culture consists not only of the musicians, the poets, the puppeteers, but also photographers, actors, writers, architects, filmmakers, sculptors, dancers, painters—the list seems endless, and comprises every creative field imaginable.

Yet as significant as Arts and Culture has been in helping people experience the liberation that comes with freedom of expression, the story of OWS and the arts must also credit those many individuals who, though unaffiliated with the working group, spontaneously appear and create on a daily basis. Even occupiers from other cities have shown up, like Jaco from Toronto who brought an array of instruments ranging from an ocarina to a drum set and who talked about the role of jamming in bringing people together. He is not the only artist to have this particular vision: ambling troubadours routinely strum a few chords, gather a crowd beneath the shade trees, and instigate group sing-alongs to classics by musicians like Bob Dylan, Woody Guthrie, the Byrds, and Buffalo Springfield. Also of note is the now infamous drum circle convened at the western edge of the park, setting what they believe is the vital heartbeat—or Pulse, as they have named themselves—of the movement.

Visual artists contribute to the community as well. Some, like James, sit and draw their surroundings. Others, like a former

Broadway garment worker, visit the park daily to sit and knit hats for the people sleeping there. Another woman, a Brooklyn artist, spends each evening at home painting something she feels is inspiring and then returns to the park the next day to show it and explain it to those around her. On nice days, a group of screen printers sets up and affixes their design of the day to any material one wishes; an especially arresting design was of the NYPD's surveillance tower as a *Robo Cop*-esque ED-209 walker, with the words "Welcome to New York" and "Occupy Wall Street" in block letters surrounding the image. Of course, amateur photographers and videographers also abound; in this digital age every one of us is an artist. Significantly, protesters take snapshots and movies both for posterity and as a way of keeping a record of NYPD behavior, as they fear police will beat occupiers or otherwise break the law.

Even writers have found a way to engage the masses surrounding them. On Thanksgiving Day, one attendee, Kat, was offered a poem by an older gentleman sitting at one of the marble tables. He had her sit while he narrated it to a young man, who scrawled it on a notepad and, when finished, tore it out for her to keep. As she walked away he was approaching another protester with the same offer. Signs are also a major vehicle for written expression. Because they are no longer allowed to carry posters with poles, activists appropriate pizza boxes from the many donated "Occupies" ordered by supporters across the country form local Liberato's Pizza. These they inscribe with slogans showcasing the diversity of voices within the park, from calls to action directed at people walking by—*If you make less than $250,000 a year you belong on this side!*—to calls for revolution—*Capitalism kills!*—to calls for reform—*Reinstate Glass-Steagall.*

The most organized of these written communications is the *Occupied Wall Street Journal* which, though not an official component of the movement, has nevertheless become an iconic part of it. Writers span the spectrum from well known, like Cornell West and Barbara Kingsolver, to unknown, and the paper publishes images, tear-out posters, editorials, and descriptions of people's experiences from across the country. Protesters play the role of paper boy both at Zuccotti Park and at all major events, carrying piles of the periodical on their forearms and offering free copies to all who walk by.

Though the physical space of Zuccotti is no longer occupied en masse, the autonomous art that emerged in the park still exists but also now "occupies" spaces in marches, protests, and even cultural centers. Local radical bookstore and activist center Bluestockings has showcased art on OWS; the music venue Southpaw is planning a concert for Occupy artists; the Epifaneo Collective, a Lower Manhattan music venue, hosts meetings for the OWS Spokes Council on Mondays and Wednesdays; another local venue holds a weekly OWS open mic. Along with the Arts and Culture working group, an Arts and Labor group has emerged and protests unfair labor practices among art handlers, production workers, and other oft exploited members of the arts workforce.

Ultimately, artists involved in the Occupy movement believe that they are simultaneously reviving both grassroots politics and grassroots arts. As Jez has argued, all of OWS's General Assemblies and official Direct Actions not only involve elements of artistic expression: the gatherings are *themselves* pieces of art. "The first performance of Occupy Wall Street was the General Assembly, actually . . . We were engaged in an act of civil disobedience," he described, while explaining how the first GAs had more than the legal limit of twenty participants allowed at public gatherings. In his opinion, that first GA and all subsequent acts of civil disobedience were "by definition performances" with facilitators and participants creating a new form of performance with an audience that both observes and participates. Alex similarly described acts of civil disobedience as

OWS-sponsored performance art—art which is, in his description, OWS engaging in a dance with the authorities. The sum of the direct actions, in his conception, is a carefully choreographed way of testing the government's limits. OWS says "[l]et's test the grounds," explained Alex, "let's put our foot there and, okay, let's see how the system reacts."

In this context, it is perhaps fitting that activist artists find themselves nestled between *Joie de Vivre*, a sinuous steel sculpture by Mark di Suvero that reaches exuberantly for the heavens and which the protesters affectionately call "The Red Thing," and the World Trade Center, one of the most significant sites in recent American history. For the hundreds of artists affiliated with OWS, and for the thousands more who participate in or sympathize with the movement, this symbolic mix of art and history makes political change seem tangible, and, as Arts and Culture member Imani Brown described it, "accessible to the people." In addition is artists' desire to bring hope - and finally Imani, like so many others, feels invigorated and "really excited" for a future already beginning to seem brighter.

The Occupation Spreads

"Bam. We're back at Oscar Grant Plaza. They spent half a million dollars to evict us, only to figure out that we won't quit. 2500 people here. Holding General Assembly."
—Facebook post by Boots Riley, musician and Occupy Oakland activist, responding to the re-encampment on October 27.

There are a thousand quiet reasons that people the world over were left rapt by the revolutions and occupations that spread throughout Northern Africa, into the Middle East and around the Mediterranean into Southern Europe in the early months of 2011. But for many in the United States, especially for those stricken with unrequited longing for the change promised by the election of Barack Obama, the news from abroad instilled a tentative new hope. Live streaming Al Jazeera on their laptops, scouring the blogs and following the Twitter feeds of occupiers from Egypt's Tahrir Square to Madrid's Puerta del Sol, many around the United States began to ask themselves an exciting question: Could this happen here?

With the occupation of Zuccotti Park in mid-September the answer to that question seemed a resounding "Yes!" And much as uprisings spread like wildfire through the Mediterranean basin, the New York spark quickly inspired occupations throughout North America and U.S. imperial territories across the globe. Also like its predecessors, oft referred to as the "Arab Spring" and "European Summer," the burgeoning Occupy movement that constituted the "American Autumn" relied on new media and social networking tools to coordinate and extend from coast-to-coast and beyond. Occupiers took to sites like Facebook and Twitter to launch events and spread the word as new occupations sprang up. Sites like OccupyTogether.com and Meetup.com proved crucial in helping far-flung participants connect and begin organizing. Maps soon showed "occupy" Facebook pages sprouting like mushrooms around the United States. Google and Twitter reported "Zuccotti" and "#OWS" to be "trending," thus magnifying the mass interest in the occupations.

By early October, occupations had materialized from Boston to Portland, Oregon from Memphis to Los Angles, from Washington D.C. to Honolulu and most everywhere in between. This proliferation of occupations was aided by the online and institutional infrastructure created by Occupy Wall Street from its base in Zuccotti. The movement's de facto (though unofficial) Web site, OccupyWallSt.org, coordinated the aims of the day and gave those who could not make it down to lower Manhattan a front-row seat to General Assemblies, demonstrations and daily life in the park via livestream video. The Twitter hash tag #needsoftheoccupiers even made it possible for supporters to identify and meet the needs of occupiers from afar—whether by ordering pizza to be delivered to Zuccotti or by shipping books to stock the People's Library. But if the widespread and effective use of social media made the Occupy movement seem somewhat streamlined and efficient, the reality on the ground was often far messier. Tools like Facebook and Twitter could coordinate the consumption of news and help establish the meeting place for events, but the business of setting agendas, prioritizing goals and facilitating discussion was an intensely intimate affair—attitudes, egos and miscommunications were not uncommon.

For many activists who traveled to Zuccotti for inspiration, either virtually or in person, establishing an occupation may have looked relatively easy. But movement building is always a far more contingent endeavor.

Take, for instance, the beginnings of Occupy Brooklyn. It should have been simple enough. Zuccotti Park was located only one mile away from the edge of New York City's most populous borough. Furthermore, Brooklyn was rife with local issues to rally against: the controversial Atlantic Yards project had recently pushed longtime residents and local business out of their homes in downtown Brooklyn; home foreclosure rates were at an abominable high; and the poverty rate was rampant. From early in the occupation of Zuccotti, Brooklyn-based occupiers had expressed interest in starting an occupation across the East River to take on some of the issues of special concern to the borough's residents. Several activists attempted to lead the charge—the problem was, they did not know one another.

"In late September a few of us that met on Twitter decided to bring the message of Occupy Wall Street to Brooklyn," Occupy Brooklyn organizer Boris Nemch recalled, "During this early stage, planning was sparse. Once we had a host location, I produced and distributed fliers, sent out Twitter blasts, spoke with media and union officials, doing anything I could to raise awareness of Occupy Wall Street." Boris said that working with people he had met online, and never in person, quickly produced challenges. "Most worked independently with minimal collaboration and communication," he said. "Which made for a sloppy process at best."

On October 13, Boris announced at an OWS organizer's dinner in Manhattan that there would be a General Assembly in Brooklyn. He and 15 to 20 other Brooklyners soon formed a breakout group, and attempted to piece together who had done what work toward organizing the Occupy movement in the borough. Spirits were high but confusion abounded. Ultimately, members of the dinner meeting breakout group, which included Alessandra De Meo, Nani Mathews, Leo Goldberg and Kara Segal, made contact with the OWS Outreach working group and designed flyers to promote a first Brooklyn General Assembly, to be held at a community space on Franklin Avenue in Crown Heights on October 20. They then canvassed, passing out fliers on street corners in Brooklyn and throughout the Zuccotti encampment.

On the evening of October 20, nearly a hundred people arrived at the dingy common space in downtown Brooklyn, and an under-trained discussion facilitator, an older, granite-haired man named Jeff, could barely contain the kinetic energy in the room. There was near-constant chatter, but strict attention was paid to process and the hastily prepared agenda. Endless discussion ensued, and the tedium drove away some attendees, their heads shaking in frustration. Three hours later, the only definitive decision that had been made was to appoint a committee to designate the time and place of the next meeting. Still, organizer and longtime Brooklyner Alessandra De Meo considered the first GA a success. "I felt relieved, excited, frustrated, angry and a bit worried as well," she said.

* * *

A Dispatch From the Pacific Northwest
By David Osborn, one of the early organizers of Occupy Portland

On September 25, a small group of people met at Powell's Bookstore to begin a conversation about calling Occupy Portland's first General Assembly. On September 30th, some 200-300 people answered this call and met in Waterfront Park. This meeting began a process that would eventually mobilize tens of thousands and bring Portland into the emerging Occupy Movement.

The spread of the movement to Portland, Seattle and other west coast cities began to pick up momentum in the week after the September 17 beginning of Occupy Wall Street.

After only two General Assemblies and less than a week of active planning, some 10,000 Portlanders gathered in Waterfront Park at noon on October 6 to stand in solidarity with Occupy Wall Street. The crowd marched to Pioneer Square before finally ending in Chapman and Lownesdale Squares which they were to occupy, with approximately 400 people, for thirty-eight days before being evicted. The eviction followed an extraordinary night of resistance during which crowds ranging from 6,000-10,000 defied and delayed the eviction for ten hours after the initial 12:01 a.m. deadline. The movement, however, was only beginning. Only four days later, on November 17, Portlanders joined people around the nation to "Occupy the Banks" and shut down the Steel Bridge and corporate banks throughout the city with thousands participating and forty-six arrested during acts of civil disobedience.

As the end of November approached the movement was spreading throughout the city. Neighborhood assemblies were being planned, relationships were being built with unions, faith groups and community organizations and a vital conversation about profit, greed, the economic crisis and the role of corporations in Portland and throughout America was well underway.

* * *

The first Brooklyn GA no doubt paralleled the initial meetings of many occupations nationwide—where strangers gathered, many not well acquainted with horizontal decision-making and the oft-tedious procedures that accompany the General Assembly format, to debate their deepest frustrations and possible solutions. "People in Brooklyn are not starting out together like people did in Manhattan," Alessandra said. "At Zuccotti, the first GAs [were] comprised of a tight homogeneous group of people who was starting out together. In Brooklyn many different people are trying to follow a model that we have not entirely claimed as our own yet." Ultimately, things got smoother and Occupy Brooklyn found its legs—establishing its own working groups and goals.

Likewise, as the Occupy movement spread, its success or failure in a particular locale was often rooted in the ability of local organizers to accommodate local conditions and articulate locally relevant issues. This was true of the movement worldwide. Cypriots occupied the United Nations-controlled buffer zone in Nicosia in order to demand an end to their island's decades-long division. Italians angered by the European Commission, the European Central Bank, and the International Monetary Fund—three institutions believed culpable for Europe's present economic woes—seized the piazzas of Rome, while Mongolian trade unionists used the movement as a means of protesting high bank interest rates, and dispossessed New Zealanders pitched tents on the site of their demolished state-funded homes. Participants of Occupy Las Vegas gambled on the movement's notoriety in a bid to fetch local businesses from the brink of foreclosure, while Occupy St. Louis demonstrators hewed to a tried-and-true method of making their voices heard, forging alliances with trade unions to stage at least two strike actions and a walkout.

With its long history of radical organizing and social protest, Oakland quickly emerged as the Occupy movement's West Coast epicenter. Naming its original encampment Oscar Grant Plaza— after a young Oakland man who had been fatally shot in the back by Bay Area Rapid Transit (BART) police officer Johannes Mehserle on New Years Day 2009—Occupy Oakland cast the local movement in direct opposition to the city's long history of police violence and repression. Local officials responded in ways that unwittingly reinforced the Occupiers' claims of endemic police brutality in the city. The Oakland camp was one of the first to be raided by police, on the evening of October 25. During that eviction, police fired tear gas canisters into the crowd, fracturing the scull of 24-year-old Marine and occupier Scott Olsen. As Olsen lay bleeding near the police barricades, and fellow protesters rushed to render aid, another officer tossed a flash grenade in his direction—violently dispersing those who rushed to Olsen's side, and sparking national condemnation, as slow-motion video of the incident rapidly circulated through YouTube. Two days later, protesters had reoccupied Oscar Grant Plaza, and a 2,000-person General Assembly called for a "General Strike" for November 2 to avenge Olsen and the park's initial eviction.

Until November 2, the "General Strike" as a tactic had been more-or-less out of use in the U.S. for more than six decades, and it was initially unclear just what would happen on that day. While the strike did not totally shut down the city, it did garner the widespread support of students, workers, labor unions, and even small business owners, some of whom closed down in solidarity with the Occupy movement. Thousands of demonstrators, with tacit solidarity from ILWU dockworkers and independent contractor port truck drivers, shut down the Port of Oakland for the evening. The success of this "General Strike" in Oakland invigorated activists across the country and the world, leading to solidarity actions by the New York occupation and others, and giving many a new sense of the possible and the power of the 99 percent. More generally, the Oakland occupation and its success helped spark debate in the camps and around the country about expanding the movement's tactics— from the occupation of new spaces, such as foreclosed homes, to the costs and benefits of "property destruction," such as graffiti and breaking windows.

* * *

A Dispatch From the Midwest
By Dan La Botz, an organizer for Occupy Cincinnati

In a bid to achieve critical mass of their own, activists in Cinncinnati staged an occupation of their own. Within two weeks of the occupation of Zuccotti Park in New York, the Occupy Wall Street movement had caught the attention of Cincinnati activists. A group of NGO staffers in the Over-the-Rhine neighborhood, longtime radical activists, and ordinary Cincinnatians began discussing the idea of establishing Occupy Cincinnati. They decided to organize Occupy Cincinnati in solidarity with Occupy Wall Street, but also planned to take on gentrification in Over-the-Rhine.

The movement began on October 8 with a march by 800 people from Lytle Park to Fountain Square in the very center of downtown Cincinnati. That night about a dozen people remained at Fountain Square after closing time despite threats of arrest by police. Dozens of other activists marched around the square in solidarity throughout the night, and when morning came, the Occupiers remained. The following day, Occupy Cincinnati moved to nearby Piatt Park, set up tents, and began holding general assemblies there every night at 6 p.m. From Piatt Park Occupiers launched marches and actions against Fifth Third Bank and local politicians.

Beginning on October 9, however, police began to issue $105 citations to those who stayed in the park after 10 p.m., leading eventually to 253 such tickets. In response, four individual plaintiffs and Occupy Cincinnati filed a Federal civil rights lawsuit on October 17, the first in the country, asserting their First Amendment right to assembly and speech in the park. Within days of the filing of the civil suit, the Cincinnati Park Board met to amend its rules to address the constitutional defects highlighted in the Occupy suit, and soon thereafter, police began arresting protesters who remained in Piatt Park and also others who re-occupied Fountain Square, leading to a total of 60 arrests. Occupy Cincinnati, still pursuing its Federal lawsuit, also challenged the constitutionality of the arrests and citations in the criminal courts.

* * *

If the occupations in New York and Oakland have commanded the most national headlines, much of the movement's growth has in fact occurred in smaller cities and towns—Las Cruces, New Mexico, Cedar Rapids, Iowa, and Providence, Rhode Island, for instance—as well as in the form of small occupations in large cities. Phoenix, Arizona stands as a particularly illuminating example of the latter. On October 14, 2011 some 200 protesters staged a "pre-occupation march" through the city's downtown financial district. Like their coastal counterparts, Phoenix marchers chanted "We are the 99 percent!" and hoisted aloft signs reading, "Speculators stole our homes," and "Bank of Me need a bailout." The march paused, now and then, to picket the local offices of Chase Bank, Bank of America and Wells Fargo before bivouacking in César Chávez Plaza at the foot of city hall, where protesters marked The Global Day of Change. The following day, hundreds more arrived to demonstrate. Though most went home soon after dusk, some remained, maintaining a round-the-clock occupation in defiance of a city ordinance that prohibits camping in public spaces. This hearty remnant, however, represented an exceedingly small minority of the movement's supporters in the area, according to one Phoenix organizer. "The Occupy movement in Phoenix is largely populated by what we call the 'Cyber99' or folks who cannot physically occupy the Plaza," she said. Arizona's status as a right-to-work state means that bosses can fire workers for no cause. As such, many otherwise willing participants were "reluctant to be physically seen at the site." Such an environment makes it "next to impossible to have a 'pure' occupation" in Phoenix, the organizer lamented. Thus, in many locales unfavorable labor laws and right-leaning electorates combined to complicate the Occupy movement's efforts to achieve the sort of critical mass necessary for political effectiveness.

But even local ordinances and unfavorable political climates did not stop smaller city occupiers from trying. Protesters in Missoula, Montana, for example, made a gesture toward civic pride when they agreed to temporarily suspend their occupation in honor of Veteran's Day, and a celebration at the site that had already been planned. Upon their return, officials told them that their camp was now limited to a small gazebo and threatened them with arrest. When they initially decided to abide by the new limitations, the local paper called them "quitters." Volunteer lawyers soon filed suit, however and the county backed down, allowing the encampment to continue in its full form. In an open letter published online, Missoula occupier Tara Hart, said "the funny thing" was, "prior to this underhanded attempted eviction, we were having very serious thoughts of decamping for Winter—we have almost no money, we have few tents, we have only one very small, partially functioning heater. But this duplicitous attempted eviction united us in a way that is impossible to describe and at tonight's GA we unanimously decided to re-encamp. We have no idea how we are going to make it, but we took what can only be characterized as a leap of faith. I've never been prouder to be a part of something in my life."

The Media, Occupied

*"Occupy Wall Street was not a media phenomenon,
it was, and is, a grass-roots combustion that happened
to have a lot of cameras pointed at it."*
—*David Carr, media columnist,* The New York Times

First, it was a near-total blackout. Then confused, on-every-channel saturation. Along the way, the media at turns sensationalized, name-called, lionized, tsked, denounced, and embraced the nascent movement. Mainstream coverage of Occupy Wall Street has been a fickle, ornery beast.

Most outlets struggled to find a clear narrative to build around OWS, while conservative cable shows and radio pundits wasted no time attacking it. Reporters were routinely roughed up, arrested, or barred from doing their jobs, and a number have lost those jobs in the process, evidently skewing too close to activism for their employers' tastes. In other words, the Occupy movement has done nothing less than test the very standards of what objective journalism should look like in a modern, free society.

The movement's notoriously rocky relationship with the media was born alongside the initial, inauspicious protests on September 17, 2011. Despite attracting a thousand or so people to lower Manhattan for a spirited march on the financial district,

Occupy Wall Street's first action drew a blind eye from the mainstream media. A mention in a couple dailies, a single blog post in the *New York Times'* City Room. Even as the protesters hauled tents to Zuccotti Park and proceeded to set up camp, few major outlets paid attention. Cameras and news vans were nowhere to be found as protesters staged marches and gained in numbers. Instead, news of Occupy spread through the blogosphere, by word-of-mouth. Michael Moore and Roseanne Barr visited Zuccotti, and helped get the occupation a little ink. But by and large, silence.

Moore went on Rachel Maddow's show on MSNBC to lambast the media blackout.

"People are down on Wall Street right now holding a sit-in and a camp-in down there," he said. "There's virtually no news about this protest. This goes on with liberals and the left all the time, and it gets ignored."

A few days later, Keith Olbermann did a comprehensive *Countdown* segment on Current TV, and a handful of articles appeared on blogs and in left-leaning outlets. And yet, outside of liberal circles, Occupy Wall Street wasn't even a blip. Until September 26, and the now infamous pepper spraying of young women protesters by the NYPD, Occupy Wall Street coverage didn't even register on the radar of Pew Research's media analysis.

This not only irked the activists, but also less involved supporters who'd discovered the movement from unconventional sources. Thus #OWS and #OCUPPYWALLST hashtags proliferated on Twitter, decrying the lack of coverage, and readers bombarded their news outlets with complaints that they were ignoring the occupation. That the media was turning a blind eye to OWS became a story unto itself. NPR would later dedicate an entire segment explaining its lack of coverage. In an article called "Newsworthy? Determining the Importance of the Protests on Wall Street," NPR's executive news editor Dick Meyer explained why they hadn't run a single story on OWS for the entire first week of its existence: "The recent protests on Wall Street did not involve large numbers of people, prominent people, a great disruption or an especially clear objective." Comments quickly appeared online pointing out that NPR had covered Tea Party rallies attended by as few as 40 people.

But it wasn't celebrity support or progressive kvetching that finally tipped the needle. It was, as is depressingly so often the case in protest movements, police brutality. News that 80 protesters had been arrested in a peaceful march to Union Square, and shocking video of four young women being casually and pointlessly pepper sprayed while corralled in a police pen, was what finally pushed Occupy Wall Street into the national news cycle. The media was left grappling with how to explain what had happened and why; why hundreds of young students were willing to brave aggressive policing and rough living conditions to march around Wall Street and camp in a park. They listened to occupiers talk about income inequality and corporate greed; they had no choice but to absorb and relay at least chunks of OWS's core message.

The media immediately felt compelled to evaluate the movement, to attempt to create a neat, overarching storyline out of its disparate elements. Pundits and opinionators began puzzling over the occupation, about who was behind, who were its spokespeople, what were its demands? The framing of the movement as a "left-wing Tea Party" was about the best the commentators on CNN, Fox, and NBC could muster.

Much of the early coverage—even the non-Fox News coverage—was downright condescending or dismissive. CNN's Erin Burnett mocked the protests in a derisive segment called 'Seriously, Protesters!?' in which she mused "What are they protesting? Nobody seems to know!" before going on to trivialize everything she saw at Zuccotti. One of the *New York Times'* first pieces on the protest, "Gunning for Wall Street with Faulty

Aim," adopted a similar tone. In it, Gina Belafonte "document-ed" the "intellectual void" of OWS and "the group's lack of co-hesion and its apparent wish to pantomime progressivism rather than practice it." She dismissed the occupation as "an opportu-nity to air societal grievances as carnival."

But there was simply too much grassroots momentum be-hind OWS for the public to lose interest, even in the face of the wave of pooh-poohing from the media's armchair pundits. The sweeping arrests of 700 protesters on the Brooklyn Bridge, fol-lowed by a union-supported march of nearly 20,000 people in Foley Square, offered unambiguous evidence that the movement was growing, and the hitherto sporadic media attention turned quickly into a deluge of around-the-clock coverage, with news vans taking up permanent station in the environs of Zuccotti.

By October 6, comedian Jon Stewart quipped that the media had "moved its coverage dial from 'blackout' to 'circus'. But those are the only two settings it has." And sure enough, Oc-cupy Wall Street was thrust front and center into the cultural zeitgeist, amidst a sea of talking heads, newspaper ink, and mag-azine covers. OWS now commanded attention at dinner table conversations, father-daughter arguments, and dorm-room de-bates across the nation.

News organizations eagerly dug in for angles, and dispatched reporters to Zuccotti to find answers to questions that contin-ued to nag: How were they organizing? How did they eat, sleep, go to the bathroom? How could there be no leaders? Were there *still* no demands?

While a bewildered mainstream media sought to make sense of the notion that, yes, a diverse coalition of people could pro-test income inequality and the rampant Wall Street greed with-out a specific policy platform, "Occupy" became a full-throttle cultural meme. The word pervaded national discourse, and metastasized into a modern riff on "protest." Clean energy ad-vocates launched 'Occupy Rooftops' to promote a solar power action, for instance, and environmentalist groups tapped into the "Occupy" aesthetic to help gather 12,000 for a protest at the White House. Less seriously, the "Occupy" meme proliferated online—football fans started "Occupy Couch," "Occupy Sesame Street" condemned monsters eating 99% of the cookies, and "Occupy the URL" filled laptop screens with images of digital protesters.

The outlets continued to binge: they ran human interest stories about the daily life in the camp, they embedded with the protesters, they obsessed over the activists' artwork and style, they profiled the occupiers. During the second week of October, 10 percent of all national news coverage was devoted to Occupy Wall Street. The movement was undeniably in the nation's bloodstream; it seemed that reporters and anchors had more trouble making sense of OWS than average Americans.

The conservative media, however, did not find it difficult to manufacture its own narrative about OWS. Fox News, the rightwing blogosphere, and radio pundits like Rush Limbaugh hastened to lay into the movement. They went to lengths to discredit OWS by focusing on fringe characters who hung around the park, playing up instances of alleged bad behavior, and claiming the whole shebang was funded by Democrats and Obama's reelection campaign.

In one segment of his cable show, Sean Hannity painted a lurid picture of the occupation for Fox News viewers: "Garbage is everywhere. The *New York Post* describes a scene where drugs are being sold, people urinating and defecating in public. By the way, there's a picture in the *Daily Mail* of one guy going to the bathroom, number 2, on a police car. You can't make this stuff up. They're passing out condoms, there's open sex, drugs are easy to score." The photo run by the *Mail* circulated extensively on rightwing blogs in an attempt to discredit the protest, though the disheveled-looking man who appeared in it was never proven to be linked to OWS.

Rush Limbaugh, predictably, out-fulminated even Fox, revealing on his radio program that "This whole thing is a construct of the media-Democrat complex, industrial complex." Karl Rove described the protesters as a "group of nuts and lunatics and fascists" and Fox host Greg Gutfield called OWS "a bunch of wusses."

The smear jobs didn't come without blowback. Fox News was famously ridiculed after it decided not to air an interview with the quick-witted protester Jesse LaGreca, who gave as good as he got in front of the microphone and went on to become one of the first, entirely unofficial media stars of OWS. "It's fun to talk to the propaganda machine and the media," LaGreca told a producer for Greta Van Sustren's show. "Especially conservative media networks such as yourself. Because we find that we can't get conversations about the Department of Justice's ongoing investigation of News Corporation, for which you are an employee. But we can certainly ask questions like you know, why are the poor engaging in class warfare?"

There were journalists, however, and more than a few, who attempted to portray the movement in a more accurate fashion. Some even came of the fence and openly sympathized with the protests they were covering. Those who did so frequently paid a heavy price. Natasha Lennard, a freelancer for the *New York Times* who reported on her arrest on the Brooklyn Bridge, was subsequently canned by her bosses for voicing support for the movement. Two NPR contractors lost their jobs for participating in OWS, though their involvement was marginal at most. Lisa Simeone, host of the entirely apolitical "World of Opera," was chastised by NPR for supporting the movement, and syndication for her show was dropped. Caitlin Curran, a freelance reporter for the WNYC/PRI's *The Takeway*, was fired after a photograph picturing her holding her boyfriend's pro OWS sign circulated online.

Both Lennard and Curran were able to share their stories

on nontraditional media, however. Curran's post "How Occupy Wall Street Cost Me My Job" on *Gawker* has registered nearly 200,000 page views. And Lennard penned a piece for *Salon* explaining that the arbitrary guidelines of what could be transmitted as fact in the mainstream media was leading her to abdicate those institutions altogether. "If the mainstream media prides itself on reporting the facts," Lennard wrote, "I have found too many problems with what does or does not get to be a fact—or what rises to the level of a fact they believe to be worth reporting—to be part of such a machine."

News coverage of OWS peaked at extraordinary levels in mid-November with the eviction of Zuccotti and the pepper spraying of peacefully protesting students while seated on the ground at UC Davis three days later. The Pew Research Center's Project for Excellence in Journalism reported that "All totaled, the Occupy Wall Street story accounted for 13 percent of the overall news during the week of November 14-20."

It wasn't just coverage of the evictions and the police confrontations that came across in these news items. OWS was also one of the primary drivers for economic coverage that week - stories dealt with the movement's messages concerning income inequality and corporate greed too. Operating an approach that eschewed the conventional media's demand for top-down, on-topic, sound bites, the Occupy movement nevertheless managed to broadcast around the nation and the world a powerful message about the way the economic system no longer adequately serves the 99%.

Perhaps it was precisely because of the evident authenticity of a movement that spurned professional spokespeople and PR-hype that its message spread so powerfully. "Occupy Wall Street was not a media phenomenon," David Carr, the *New York Times* media columnist, wrote on November 20, "it was, and is, a grass-roots combustion that happened to have a lot of cameras pointed at it."

Those cameras were not present, however, during the NYPD's military-style operation to clear Zuccotti in the early hours of the morning of November 15. Reporters were blocked off from covering the event, and airspace above the park was closed to news copters. Mayor Bloomberg described this move as an effort to "protect the members of the press" from the raid he himself had instigated. And so, an occupation that had begun with a comprehensive media blackout ended in the midst of another.

Eviction

"Mic check! MIC CHECK! Something horrible is happening here! SOMETHING HORRIBLE IS HAPPENING HERE!"
—*The People's Microphone, Zuccotti Park, 2 a.m., November 15*

At 12:45 a.m. on November 15, all was calm and still. The moon shone through light cloud cover, and campers huddled in tents, safe from the cool air. Outside the encampment, boots shuffled as swarms of police in riot gear took their strategic positions, then flood lamps lit up the sky to midday–rousing even the heaviest sleepers. Recorded loudspeakers blared, and cops barked orders to vacate the premises immediately.

For those not sleeping in Zuccotti, the text came at 12:59 a.m., interrupting conversations, pausing books and streaming video, and provoking naked and pajama-draped arms to reach up from beds and couches toward the screens of phones glowing in the dark early morning:

"OccupyNYC: URGENT: Hundreds of police mobilizing around Zuccotti. Eviction in progress!"

From across the city they descended–one by one, two by two, group by group, coalescing into hundreds. Many walked, some over the bridge from Brooklyn. Others arrived by bike; still others exited subway trains and hastily paid cabs. Within an hour of the initial call, those gathering at Broadway to the north of Zuccotti found scores of police and barricades at Cortlandt Street–close enough to see the massive red *Joie de Vivre* sculpture in the park's southeast corner, but too far away to witness what was happening to those who remained inside.

A group of bike activists had received a call slightly earlier, around midnight, just as their meeting was winding to a close. "There is a huge buildup of police in East River Park," the caller said, and a small group rode down. Worries about a raid had come and gone for weeks–they knew what such a build up meant. Riding downtown, they glided past hundreds of police assembled near Maiden Lane. By the time the bicyclists got to Zuccotti, a little past midnight, there was no place to park. Some tried to lock their bikes on Broadway, but a cop said, "I wouldn't park it here. If you can't figure it out, use your eyes." Looking up, an activist saw an officer in riot gear with a baton in her hand. This was it–the eviction. They watched as police surrounded the park and switched on the flood lamps.

Inside the park, police with megaphones shouted, "Please get out of the park," while passing out leaflets explaining that they were clearing the park. "Whose park? Our Park!" some responded. Others started gathering their possessions. Many reported feeling disoriented by the NYPD's use of loud sound devices.

One videographer stood filming in the middle of Cedar Street, facing the park. "For your safety, we're asking you to move," police demanded. "I don't see why I have to move," said citizen journalist Barbara Ross. "I am not scared. I am not blocking anything. I know my rights." For the next two hours, she filmed cops pepper spraying resisters, trashing library books, wrecking the park's sacred space, and completely demolishing the two-month encampment. Two female officers eventually forced Barbara behind barricades on Trinity Place, where she could no longer witness the destruction.

The cops fenced off the park: by 1 a.m. no one was allowed past the barricades. A wall of riot police corralled those inside and pushed a group of onlookers to Liberty and Broadway, a block away, where they couldn't see the wreckage. *The New York Times* and some other media had managed to sneak into Zuccotti before the raid, but officers at the barricades refused all press passes except NYPD press credentials. Police arrested six journalists and barred countless others from entering or witnessing the scene. An older man, sporting the bright green "Legal Observer" hat of the National Lawyer's Guild, claimed the raid violated not only the First Amendment right to assemble, but also the right to observe, as the police had strategically placed the barricades so as to force almost all watchful eyes to a blind periphery.

Some cyclists, hoping to save the bike-powered generators that the Sustainability Committee had installed weeks before the raid, pressed the police line only to be pushed back–one was arrested. As the crowd grew and vans marked "Sanitation" worked their way past, police pepper sprayed large swathes of protesters and reporters. "Move! Move! Move!" shouted a phalanx of helmeted, baton-wielding officers–literally pushing the crowd north of Fulton Street, where the police erected new barricades. Chants rang out: "Shame! Shame! Shame!" and "This! Is! A peaceful protest!" But the advancing wall of police and loud sound devices confused and disoriented the protesters, who could only guess what exactly was taking place in the floodlit park. "The most upsetting thing was watching the tents get taken away," a woman mused as she left the park, sleeping bag in hand. "Mic check! MIC CHECK! Something horrible is happening here! SOMETHING HORRIBLE IS HAPPENING HERE!" someone shouted, using the crowd's voices to amplify his own. "When are you guys going to protect the people?" a man asked an officer. "Just doing their jobs ruining democracy," a photographer remarked, as police shoved onlookers another block from the park. "I think this could shut down the city," a man called out to everyone in earshot. "It's already shutting down Broadway. There are like 500 people in the streets right now!"

"Whose streets? Our streets!" some hollered. "We are the 99 percent!" another group yelled, blocking traffic on Broadway. The police spent the rest of the night pushing people farther away, even forbidding them to occupy the sidewalks. When asked about what was happening inside the barricades, one officer answered, "They're clearing out Zuccotti Park . . . 'cause they've been there for two months." It was "just time to go," another added. "Just following orders?" an activist screamed. "Yep," the officer replied. "Just like the Nazis did?" the activist asked. "Yep," the officer said, matter-of-factly.

After a few hundred had gathered, a young male voice rang out: "Mic check! MIC CHECK! Mic check! MIC CHECK! We are going to! WE ARE GOING TO! Rally! RALLY! At City Hall! AT CITY HALL! Backup plan! BACKUP PLAN! Foley Square! FOLEY SQUARE! We need to get together! WE NEED TO GET TOGETHER! So we can march in force! SO WE CAN MARCH IN FORCE! Thank you! THANK YOU!" Somewhere in the crowd a woman yelled, "Let's go!" and the mass marched up Broadway to the chant of, "All day! All week! Occupy Wall Street!" then, "We! Are! The 99 percent!" before settling on the call-and-response: "Whose streets!? Our streets!"

The chants soon echoed off the walls of City Hall, as screaming sirens and the rat-tat-tat of churning helicopter blades lent a soft cacophonous soundtrack to the makeshift march. From Broadway, marchers veered right on Chambers Street and proceeded up Lafayette toward Foley Square–the site of the massive Community and Labor Rally that had bolstered the movement on October 5. In hot pursuit, the NYPD dispatched more than a dozen flashing vans, packed with cops. The police caravan halted along Chambers Street as the protesters careened onto

Lafayette, and dozens of officers wielding nightsticks rushed into Foley right behind them.

The marchers soon found themselves in the center of Foley Square, debating their next moves as riot police clogged the surrounding streets. Perched high on the fountain at the square's center, a protester hollered, "Mic check! MIC CHECK! Okay, if we stay here! IF WE STAY HERE! The police know where we are! THE POLICE KNOW WHERE WE ARE! If we keep moving! IF WE KEEP MOVING! We stay one step ahead! WE STAY ONE STEP AHEAD! I think we should keep moving! I THINK WE SHOULD KEEP MOVING! Unless anyone has their tents with them! UNLESS ANYONE HAS THEIR TENTS WITH THEM!"

Following his call, a curt public service announcement relayed the phone number of the National Lawyer's Guild, which several marchers scrawled on their forearms with pen or sharpie. After briefly debating whether to stay or to move on, about half the crowd filed out of the park, west on Worth Street, before heading north on Broadway. At nearly every turn, the police made chase—insisting protesters stick to the sidewalks, making intermittent arrests, and fragmenting the march. Some protesters wound up near Washington Square, some near Union Square, and others re-converged at Foley.

Meanwhile, at 3 a.m. hundreds of displaced occupiers and protesters were still holding their ground on Broadway at Pine. Blocked by barricades and armored police, they watched in stunned silence as cops and sanitation workers filled a steady line of dump trucks and drove off into the night. "My house is in that dump truck!" yelled one man. "They're stealing our shit!" cried another, while over the barricades, a lone troubadour played tenor guitar and sang Bob Dylan's "When The Ship Comes In." Elsewhere, chants rang out, "You're sexy! You're cute! Take off that riot suit!" and "Tell me what democracy looks like! This is what democracy looks like!"

Under the dump truck engines' growl and the crowd's din, journalists interviewed the displaced campers, while protesters tried to reconcile themselves with what had happened and speculated about the future. Occupiers chatted in between texts and phone calls–reassuring friends and loved ones who wanted to know where they were and if they were safe. They also exchanged texts with fellow protesters at Foley Square and scattered throughout the streets of lower Manhattan. Still others climbed and scribbled on police cars, and some inventive activists squatted along a line of police vehicles and used their bike gear to let the air out of the tires in one fell swoosh.

Near 5 a.m., when the dump trucks had carried off the bulk of the park's contents, the police made their push to re-open Broadway. Just behind the police line, three punk-clad protesters hooted and whistled at a young blonde female officer. She gritted her teeth. Flanking her, two male officers, both a head taller than she, stared down the catcallers in disgust. Later, one of the catcallers met the blonde officer's eyes, as if to say, "I'm sorry." As she calmly walked him out of the street, the two chatted–she about her usual beat in upper Manhattan, he about the eviction call from Brooklyn.

Meanwhile, as scores of officers pressed the restless crowd south, a muddled announcement cautioned: "If you don't leave the street, you will be arrested!" Several protesters responded by loudly humming Star Wars' "The Imperial March," which gave way to the chant, "All day! All week! Occupy Wall Street!" The chant started out slowly, almost half-time, but quickened as the NYPD swept the street. Altercations arose as the police line surged, pushing everyone out of the street and to the sidewalk outside Trinity Churchyard. Some protesters pressed back, until a swarm of officers overpowered them. Others hurled bottles and larger objects from afar. One young man leapt onto a police cruiser and hurled himself into a crowd of police. Cries rang out: "Fascists!" "Who are you protecting!?" and "Shame!" Other protesters called on the police to join them: "They're stealing your pensions too!" some shouted. But within a matter of minutes police had reclaimed Broadway. When the street was cleared and those who defied the police were arrested and gone, some cops had to change their deflated tires, which blocked morning traffic for an additional thirty minutes. As traffic resumed, those remaining made their way to Foley Square, where a General Assembly was already debating the movement's next steps.

By 6 a.m., the throngs of protesters had dispersed. Only a few dozen remained, lingering among the police and reporters chasing that perfect, post-raid sound bite. By then the barricades had thinned, making it possible to see the sanitation and security workers scrubbing every inch of the emptied park. Officers stood by, assuring the crowd that they could return within minutes, as soon as the crews finished cleaning. This turned out to be false–no one was allowed to re-enter the park until after 5 p.m. that day. Later reports revealed that most of the cops hadn't been informed about the raid. They thought they were donning riot gear as part of "an exercise," until they heard the orders to head downtown.

As the sun rose, police corralled the remaining protesters onto one sectioned-off area of the sidewalk. A few were arrested for refusing to move from the barricaded eastern sidewalk to the barricades on the west side of Broadway.

City officials were quick with their public relations–calling the eviction necessary for non-specific "health and safety" concerns and spinning negative press with silver linings. Answering initial reports of the destruction of over 5,000 People's Library books, Mayor Bloomberg quickly tweeted that all of the books were secure and would be available for recovery the following day. The truth, it seems, lies somewhere in between. Early in the morning of the raid, the Library Twitter account transmitted the following message: "The NYPD has destroyed everything at #OccupyWallStreet and put it all in dumpsters, including the

#OWS library. Its time to #ShutDownNYC." Stephen Boyer had lived in Zuccotti Park for most of the two-month encampment, worked in its library, and helped create the massive OWS poetry anthology with anonymous to famous contributors from around the world. That night, he said, he could barely save the massive anthology, before cops shoved him out of the park, and he watched them dump books into the backs of trucks. "Our library had over nine thousand books, and a little less than five thousand were taken that night," he said, adding that the rest of the books were stored in a nearby space lent to the movement. "I saved the anthology by strapping both [folders] to my back, and read from it during the raid." When asked about the incident, Bill from the People's Library added that the on-site computers, which the city also claimed were recoverable after the raid, had been "systematically destroyed." A week after the eviction, representatives of the People's Library and the lawyer they retained to sue the city, issued a press release stating that only 1,275 books were recovered, with only 839 of these in readable condition. The city, they said, had trashed or destroyed more than 3,000 of the books seized.

But if the facts of the eviction were slow to emerge, one thing was perfectly clear as the sun rose on that cool November morning. For the first time in nearly two months, Zuccotti Park was empty, but for a handful of sanitation workers and armored police. In a press conference that morning, Mayor Bloomberg chastised the occupiers for having over-stayed their welcome–for failing to exercise "responsibility" along with their rights. "Now they'll have to occupy the space with the power of their arguments," he said. As he spoke, the protesters prepared to do just that and more.

The Future of the Occupation

"It's your kids' future! You're defending your children.
That is a primal and huge thing . . . Families have to be
involved in order for this movement to continue."
—*Kirby Desmarais, founder of Parents for Occupy Wall Street*

At 6:30 a.m. on November 15, a Manhattan Supreme Court judge, Lucy Billings, signed a temporary restraining order, permitting protesters to return to Zuccotti Park. But city officials ignored the ruling and kept the park clear. When an older woman waved a copy of the court ruling at police guarding the park, a cop punched her in the face.

The park was not reopened until 5 p.m., after the city received a more favorable court ruling that banned tents and sleeping bags from the park. That evening, the public was allowed to enter a defanged Zuccotti, fenced off with barricades, except for one heavily monitored entrance and exit. While the occupation continued, its continued physical presence is tenuous at best.

No one doubted that the loss of Zuccotti Park would have a profound impact on Occupy Wall Street. Some claimed the eviction was a blessing in disguise, as the occupation faced the approach of General Winter, as well as growing burnout, assaults in the private tents, and mental illness–all real problems, but also easily exploited by those looking to discredit the movement. The day before the raid, *Adbusters* had floated the idea of ending the encampments, declaring victory, and using "the winter to brainstorm, network, build momentum so that we may emerge rejuvenated with fresh tactics, philosophies, and a myriad projects ready to rumble next Spring."

The police and Mayor Bloomberg claimed victory for the principles of obedience and respect for the status quo. Their raid took part in a national effort by 18 mayors of major U.S. cities in conjunction with federal authorities from the department of Homeland Security–a detail that Oakland Mayor Jean Quan let slip in a November 16 interview with the BBC.

Nonetheless, the takeover and transformation of a corporate plaza had given a physical address to a widespread mood of rebellion. Zuccotti Park had provided a literal home for hundreds and a political one for tens of thousands, perhaps more.

At the time of this writing, it remained unclear how the Occupy movement would evolve without the physical space that defined it from the beginning.

While the eviction's timing and ferocity caught them by surprise, occupiers and supporters had already prepared alternatives in the event that full-time occupation of Zuccotti Park became impossible. Attempting to evade police crackdowns and to extend the occupation in time and space, protesters sought sites whose owners or managers supported the movement and were willing to be occupied–or, at least, unwilling to remove an occupation with force.

On October 16, a few dozen occupiers tried to expand the occupation to a "friendly" site at the Guggenheim Lab on Houston Street and Second Avenue. A public event at this location almost grew into a full-time indoor encampment, but this OWS satellite collapsed when occupiers resisted the owner's request that they coordinate security for the site. One month later, hours after the eviction from Zuccotti, a flurry of texts, Twitters and

Facebook posts directed protesters to convene at 9 a.m. at Canal Street and Sixth Avenue. They were greeted by a contingent of clergy who supported the movement and its message against inequality. A few hundred occupiers scaled chain-link fences to occupy a disused triangle of land at the mouth of the Holland Tunnel. Trinity Church, one of New York City's largest real estate holders, owned this property. When the clergy couldn't negotiate an ongoing occupation with Trinity, riot cops moved in and dispersed the camp.

In conjunction with the November 17 National Day of Action, students coordinated a more successful search for a new, full-time occupation space occurred. The students met for "lunch" at a student rally at Union Square–the destination of citywide feeder marches and speakouts. From there, a breakout march entered and "occupied" a New School University Building on 5th Avenue. Marchers heading to Foley Square saw signs in the window declaring the space "occupied!" The quest for "friendly" hosts briefly succeeded. The New School, founded by left-wing professors fleeing Nazi repression in Germany, initially tolerated the burgeoning All-City Student Occupation–perhaps reasoning that an eviction would mar its reputation as a progressive institution. But relations between the protesters and administration soon frayed over issues like graffiti and fire codes, and when the president tried to persuade the occupiers to move to a new space at the New School, their General Assembly passed the proposal with a 75% majority, though dissenters from the proposal chose to stay and continue the occupation. The question of how to deal with a tolerant host—a problem those still in Zuccotti would love to have—actually split this occupation, and by the end of the Thanksgiving weekend the last holdouts had voluntarily disbanded.

At the time of this writing, Zuccotti remains occupied during the day, but at night protesters must leave. A sympathetic hotel owner in the Rockaways shelters many at night, but it's a long commute every day, back and forth to the global finance capital. The logistical hassles of the eviction have exacerbated tensions over myriad issues from money to gluten-free food.

Nonetheless, along with efforts to expand to new physical spaces, Occupy's energy and memes have spread to a wide array of political spaces and campaigns. The movement has contributed bodies and support to many causes. Protesters have "occupied" foreclosed homes and homes facing foreclosure in Minneapolis, Oakland, Portland, Cleveland and other cities. They have occupied the Department of Education in New York, by holding protests, teach-ins and discussions on how to reform the system so that it works for students, teachers and parents and not for the privatization lobby. They have occupied student debt—collecting and sharing stories of debt-related hardship on a Web site and starting a campaign to refuse crippling loan repayments predicated on unjust interest rates. They have held joint rallies with unions and lent their bodies and energy to pickets and labor actions. They have offered assistance to immigrants, in one case helping to fight a deportation by organizing a march and publicizing a rally.

These examples, along with countless others, suggest a wholesale reinvigoration of protest in the U.S. Campaigners who have struggled for years to engage public interest are now receiving extra support and publicity through the eye-catching Occupy brand, its numbers and determination, and last but not least, its irresistibly inclusive "99 Percent" slogan. As *Atlantic* commentator Alexis Madrigal pointed out, the Occupy concept resembles an Application Programming Interface from a Web site—a kind of framework for integrating the disparate into a whole. No one can deny the tensions within OWS and the broader Occupy movement, but so far a shared analysis and common language has bound the different strands together.

But at what point does integration become co-optation? What would constitute co-optation by the Democratic party and other mainstream liberal organizations, and what would constitute support? Within the first month of the Occupation, Democrats from Al Gore to Nancy Pelosi to the president himself expressed sympathy for the protesters' concerns. Some Democrat-friendly groups, such as the Center for American Progress, have shown interest in using OWS for voting drives. Not long after Gore's endorsement, Salon commentator Glenn Greenwald lit into Mary Kay Henry, the president of SEIU (one of the unions most supportive of Obama and the Democrats) for co-opting the language and slogans of Occupy to rally support for Obama's re-election campaign. In an interview with the *Washington Post*'s Greg Sargent, Henry had promoted the notion of "Occupy Congress" and set up a false dichotomy in which occupiers and unions would side with the Democrats against Republicans. Yet everyone, especially OWS, knows that the Grand Old Party is not the only "party of the rich." Occupy protesters may well "Occupy Congress"–but not in the way Henry and other Obama supporters imagine. As Greenwald pointed out, what makes Occupy so pertinent is its resolve to work outside of corrupt political institutions. Appropriating the movement for a Democratic campaign would simply make Occupy another voting arm–and either narrow its appeal or kill it.

David Carr contended that getting people elected and pressuring for legislative demands is still how things get done, however unsatisfactorily. Yet, our elite political system, allied with corporate interests, sparked the protests in part. In order to get its messages across and enact change, Occupy will have to use all tools available. Engaging in the existing political process may well be one; yet any involvement in electoral politics must surely be on Occupy's own terms.

Despite the complex questions of building a broad coalition, the bigger challenge could still be evading the authorities and dealing with increasing police brutality.

As OWS moves forward, changing location, shape and

tactics, the militarization of the New York City Police Department, its capacity and willingness to use excessive force, remains a significant obstacle for developing new sites of protest and new tactics.

Sociologist and Brooklynite Alex Vitale describes how YouTube images of NYPD and Davis riot police pepper-spraying peaceful protesters became possible. After a long period of "negotiated management" between protesters and police during the 1970s and 80s, the Seattle Police Department's perceived failure to stem the 1999 Battle in Seattle, followed closely by the terror attacks in 2001, gave police departments both the motivation and the excuse to militarize. Vitale argues that legacy of New York Mayor Rudolph Giuliani's "broken-windows" policing and "quality of life" can be seen in NYPD's micromanagement of OWS and related demonstrations. When protesters defy minor rules, NYPD falls back on overwhelming force as it did during the first Brooklyn Bridge march.

It remains to be seen what the balance of physical and political force will mean for the future of OWS and the #occupy movement. Police departments, armed with an array of crowd control technologies, have the capacity to disperse unarmed encampments and crowds. And big-city, mostly-liberal mayors have shown their willingness to work together to try to take on protesters. But harsh tactics have backfired, causing public relations problems for police and politicians. So far the #occupy movement has responded to police brutality, above all, by growing.

Will police and politicians continue cracking down, change tactics, or return to the old days of "negotiated settlement?" Will #occupy remain defiant and grow?

There are many signs that it can. For one thing, the Occupy movement appeals to constituencies far beyond the stereotypical image of "protesters." One cold day in November, amid the cacophony of unsanctioned drumming and Reverend Billy's protest against Goldman Sachs, a suburban couple, both pediatricians with three kids, explained that they had come to attend the General Assembly meeting. Though many in their Westchester town had lowered their flags to half-mast when Barack Obama was elected president, Ivanya Alpert and her husband, Dmitri Laddis, see Occupy as a sign that a more promising politics is emerging. They are tired of their kids' class sizes growing, due to budget cuts, as rapidly as their neighbors expand their McMansions. Their local public pool was sold off to a private bidder because the town couldn't afford to keep it open every summer. Alpert and Laddis spent their one date night of the year in Zuccotti Park.

A group called Parents for Occupy Wall Street, which began with a Family Sleep-Over in Zuccotti Park in October, quickly became a national phenomenon, reaching as far as Honolulu. Founded by 25-year-old Brooklyn music industry entrepreneur Kirby Desmarais, the mother of a 19-month old daughter, the group will go on tour in 2012, to educate fellow parents about the OWS movement. Desmarais, never politically active before, explained why parents have to be part of OWS: "It's your kids' future! You're defending your children. That is a primal and huge thing . . . Families have to be involved in order for this movement to continue."

Children and parents weren't the only unexpected visitors to Zuccotti and its sister encampments nationwide. Oakland police severely wounded a protesting former Marine who'd served two tours in Iraq; other veterans have been a strong presence at Occupy sites, and rightly so, given their high rates of unemployment. Perhaps even more surprisingly, in mid-November, Ray Lewis, a retired police captain from Philadelphia, was arrested in Zuccotti Park, carrying a sign that said, "NYPD Don't Be Wall Street Mercenaries." He explained his analysis of police labor: "All the cops, they're just workers for the one percent and they don't even realize it. . . . As soon as I get out of jail, I'm coming right back and they'll have to arrest me again. " This was a long way from the dream of a revolution in which military and police turn against the state, but it showed that Occupy was hardly, in Dmitri Laddis's words, "a marginal little protest."

Occupy Wall Street has consistently defied predictions and surprised self-styled trendtrackers. This summer, as the Adbusters call circulated, most activists and observers laughed at the very idea of occupying Wall Street. Canadians are calling for a camp-out on Wall Street! The police would clear it out within hours! How naïve to think people could get away with such a thing! But so far, history has proven these naysayers wrong. As the protesters declared in face of Bloomberg's second eviction, "You can't evict an idea."

Day in the Life of the Square

"THIS IS A SIGN"
—*Written on a sign in Zuccotti Park*

Morning

Administrative life at Occupy Wall Street began not at Zuccotti Park, but at the large atrium located at 60 Wall Street (where the group that created this book held its meetings). There, coordinators from the movement's various working groups met daily, and delivered reports on ongoing initiatives, discussed proposals, and brainstormed solutions. At an October 31 morning meeting, for example, the question of how to prepare the encampment for winter weather topped the meeting agenda, followed by discussion concerning the newly-formed Spokes Council and unflattering reports about the General Assembly appearing in the media.

Meanwhile, back at the encampment in Zuccotti, the various operations that kept the camp functioning were already underway. Breakfast was prepared in the People's Kitchen, starting at about 6 am, and was ready to eat about an hor later. While mealtimes became more tightly defined during the occupation's last three weeks, a steady stream of donations from local establishments, including pizza parlors and Indian restaurants, as well as food from OWS supporters who had, on their own initiative, prepared dishes in their homes, ensured that those wishing to eat could find food at almost any time of day. As the morning got going, the People's Library began receiving visits, as did the Information Desks at either end of the park, with locals and tourists stopping to talk to protesters.

On an average day, Daniel Levine arrived at Occupy Wall Street at around 10 or 11 a.m., depending on whether he had to attend one of the two college classes in which he was enrolled. His routine was simple—he would get coffee from one of the vendors around the park, and then go to the Information Desk, From that point on, he would answer questions from passersby. When there was a lull at the desk, he would read.

Lunch, like breakfast, was a freeform affair, with volunteers whisking vegetarian food on trays around the camp to members of working groups operating continually throughout the day. The staff at the Information Desk were one such group, and, sometimes, Dan availed himslef of this service. However, by his account, when he was in the mood for meat, he took a break from working at the desk and turned to the Halal trucks parked around the outside of the square. Indeed, over the course of Dan's time at the occupation—53 days, he estimated—he had availed himself of this latter option often enough to be able to offer advice on which were the best trucks to patronize. The truck on the south edge of the park, he suggested, produced the better food, but another one, located on the other side of Broadway, was cheaper.

Afternoon

The period from noon till 2 p.m. represented the first of the two, two-hour windows of time during which the drummers of

PULSE could play, according to an agreement that they had made with the General Assembly. Drumming, in due course, filled the air, most especially along the western end of the park. Nearby, Hermes, an 18-year-old native of Mobile, Alabama would be seated at a small table along the southernmost walkway, passing out leaflets containing information about the economic ills faced by the world. His typical day consisted of conversing with pass-ersby and exchanging ideas for hour after hour, until he could no longer make the effort, at which point he would go to bed.

By way of contrast, afternoons for Patricia, a participant in the Direct Action working group , usually meant leaving not just her desk, but Zuccotti Park altogther—typically groups like the one she worked in held their meetings either in the nearby atrium of 60 Wall Street or at Charlotte's Place, a gathering space operated by Trinity Wall Street, an Episcopal parish, several blocks away from the park. Usually Patricia was busy at these planning meetings until around 7 p.m., when she would return to the square in time to attend the evening's General Assembly. In the meantime, PULSE thundered its way through the second of its alloted two-hour drumming sessions, which stretched from 4 till 6 p.m. though, as many occupiers drily noted, it often over-ran so that a barrage of percussion competed with the General Assembly's mic checks.

For a short period in early November, the GA twitter-re-porter DiceyTroop, found himself between jobs. During this time, his afternoon routine was much like Patricia's: at 2 p.m., he usually tried to attend the Direction Action working group meetings in 60 Wall Street, followed at 4 p.m. by the Facilita-tion working group's meeting, followed in turn at 6 p.m. by a meeting of the Structure working group—a group that achieved particular importance within the Occupy movement from late October on, as it was in this group that the Spokes Council took shape. By the time this meeting was over it was, once again, time for General Assembly.

Evening

Dinner time in Zuccotti commenced, as a rule, around 6pm, with cooked, mostly vegetarian fare coming out of the People's Kitchen. Notwithstanding the more-or-less permanent presence of food in the Occupy camp, dinner was an important occasion for the occupiers, and, when the Kitchen faced delays, occupiers often got testy. On November 8th, for instance, Rich, a military veteran working security for the People's Kitchen who was responsible for ensuring that only authorized persons entered the area where the food was being prepared, found himself in an altercation with a kitchen volunteer as a result of frustration on the part of hungry occupiers. On that day, Rich was standing at the entrance to the kitchen, where he felt he needed to be if he was to prevent anyone unauthorized from entering. However this meant he could not avoid also obstructing kitchen volunteers. Tensions were already high: 6 p.m had passed, the food the kitchen had been expecting had not arrived yet (no one knew why), and occupiers waiting in the food line were growing impatient. Water, too, was in short supply. Rich and an anonymous kitchen worker became invloved in a tense stand off—the worker because he considdered Rich to be the in the way and refusing to move, Rich because he felt hounded by the worker, and believed he needed to stand where he was in order to properly do his job. Ultimately, the pair were forced to turn to a mediator, who settled the argument, but not without some lingering resentment.

The General Assembly generally started at around 7pm, though sometimes earlier. When it ended was another matter—the consensus process on which the GA operated was one that, at times, required lengthy negotiation between a participants who had seriously divergent opinions concerning a given measure. This was especially likely if any GA attendee placed a block on a proposal, though this happened only rarely. Meetings would often stretch beyond the four hour maximum allocated to them so that only the hardiest of attendees were present at their end.

As Hermes' recollections suggest, some of Occupy Wall Street's activities camp could not be neatly circumscribed by a particular period. Protest sign-making and other artistc endeavors took place pretty much at any time . Speakers seeking a crowd showed up throughout the day. The media center operated for long hours, the medical center was open all the time, and the long, byzantine process of resolving the legal situations of arrested OWS protesters could drag on over several days. But despite all this, the extent to which life in the park had a predictable schedule and rhythm was remarkable.

Night

As the evening wore on, depending on what sorts of protests had taken place that day, any number of Occupy Wall Street protesters might be busy at various sites across the city—busy, that is, getting released from police precincts, where they were met by OWS Legal working group-organized jail support teams.

At Zuccotti Park, meanwhile, occupiers chatted in the square or, as DiceyTroop sometimes did after finishing his tweeting of the General Assembly, might head over to a nearby bar or coffee shop—"where the real work gets done", as he put it—to discuss and plan. For those remaining in the park, one final meal was sometimes available: on many nights, an OWS supporter came around at 11 p.m. with vegan food for anyone who wanted it.

Fittingly, perhaps, given the centrality it assumed in the public image of the Occupy encampment, the People's Library typically operated late, staying open 2 or 3 in the morning, at which time Bill Scott, a professor of English spending his sabbatical as one of the Library's custodians, could at last bed down, curling up in his sleeping bag among the books as a means of safeguarding them.

Dan Levine typically stayed seated behind Info Desk East until even later—sometimes, he got on the subway back to Brooklyn as late as 5 a.m. But, according to him, these were not dead hours for the movement, even if most occupiers, and most certainly the public that streamed by during the day, were fast asleep. Late at night was when the truly interested, and interesting,individuals approached his desk. It was then that he felt like the concierge at a hotel, he said, listening to the stories people tell at odd hours of the night, something this "lover of stories" was happy to do.

Timeline of a Movement on the Move

January 25—Over 50,000 protesters took over **Tahrir Square** in **Egypt,** impairing the area's wireless services. This marked the beginning of the Egyptian revolution.

May 5—Protests in **Greece** were sparked by plans to cut public spending and raise taxes as austerity measures in exchange for a €110 billion bail-out, aimed at solving the 2010–2011 Greek debt crisis.

May 15—**Spanish** protests began in 58 cities. Protesters referred to themselves as the **Indignados.** The **Puerta del Sol** square in **Madrid** became a focal point and a symbol during the protests. The movement drew inspiration from 2011 revolutions in Tunisia, Egypt and Greece in 2008.

May 25—Anti-austerity protesters organized by the **Direct Democracy Now!** movement, known as the **Indignant Citizens Movement** started demonstrating in major cities across **Greece.**

This second wave of demonstrations was nonpartisan and began through peaceful means. Some of the protests later turned violent, particularly in the capital city of **Athens**.

June 16—Creation of **Bloombergville** at Broadway and Park in Manhattan as a direct response to Mayor Bloomberg's budget cuts.

July 13—*Adbusters*, a **Canadian** anti-consumerist magazine, made the initial call for a peaceful demonstration to occupy Wall Street.

August 2—Gathering of the General Assembly at the Charging Bull in lower **Manhattan** to protest Bloomberg's budget cuts.

August 9—General Assembly at the Irish Potato Famine Memorial (NYC)

September 1—Nine protesters were arrested for performing a peaceful occupation of **Tompkins Square** in Manhattan.

September 17—Taking of Zuccotti Park in **Manhattan**. Original target was Chase Manhattan Plaza, but police got wind of the plans and barricaded the area; Zuccotti was plan B.

September 20—A small occupation in **San Francisco** put out a call for more people to join.

September 21—OWS stood in solidarity with movements in **Madrid, San Francisco, Los Angeles, Madison, Toronto, London, Athens, Sydney, Stuttgart, Tokyo, Milan, Amsterdam, Algiers, Tel Aviv, Portland**, and **Chicago**. Occupations in **Phoenix, Montreal, Cleveland**, and **Atlanta** were beginning to form.

September 23—Similar movements appeared in **Palestine, Kansas City, Dallas, Orlando**, and **Miami**.

September 26—Noam Chomsky announced his solidarity with Occupy Wall Street.

October 5—Thousands took to the streets in **Greece** in general protest to bailouts and budget cuts.

October 6—About 5,000 protesters marched in **Portland**, Oregon. More demonstrations were held in **Los Angeles** and **San Francisco**, California; **Tampa**, Florida; **Houston** and **Austin**, Texas; and **Salt Lake City**, Utah.

October 9—A crowd of approximately 100 protesters gathered in **Washington, D.C.**, outside the White House.

October 10—Police reported that more than 140 protesters from the **Occupy Boston** movement were arrested after they ignored warnings to move from a downtown greenway near where they have been camped out for more than a week.

October 15—**Global Day of Action**. Rallies took place in over a thousand cities around the world. The date was chosen to coincide with the five-month anniversary of the first protest in **Spain**. In **Rome**, the protests turned violent after rioters hijacked a peaceful gathering causing an estimated $1.4 million of damage. In **Vancouver**, where the idea for the Occupy movement was first promoted, around 4,000 people participated, the highest turnout in **Canada**.

October 22—Dozens of protesters from **Occupy Harlem** were arrested for marching on Harlem's 28th precinct.

October 25—**Egyptian** activists who helped topple former dictator Hosni Mubarak lent their support to the growing Occupy movement, releasing a statement in solidarity with occupiers. In **Oakland,** California, hundreds of police moved against Occupy Oakland protesters, launching teargas, beanbag rounds, and rubber bullets before clearing out an encampment and arresting 85 people. Scott Olsen, an Iraq War veteran from the U.S. Marines was in critical condition after he was hit in the head with a police projectile.

October 26—**Oakland Solidarity** march. Hundreds of OWS protesters marched near Union Square in support of Iraq War veteran and Occupy Oakland protester Scott Olsen.

October 27—Jean Quan, mayor of Oakland, said the Occupy Oakland protesters could stay, in the wake of Tuesday's violent police eviction of the encampment in front of City Hall.

October 28—Occupy Wall Street joined with **Occupy the Hood** to take action against illegal foreclosure practices.

October 29—Tensions flared in **Denver,** Colorado near the State Capitol when police entered the campsite. There were reports of skirmishes between police and protesters, with more than a dozen arrests. A group of protesters characterized as "thugs" surrounded and pushed over a police motorcycle while the policeman was riding it. The police dispersed the OWS protesters by firing rounds of pellets filled with pepper spray.

October 30—Police arrested two-dozen people in **Portland,** Oregon, for failing to leave a park when it closed at midnight. Police arrested 38 people in **Austin,** Texas after they refused to put away food tables at 10 p.m. Those arrested contested the legitimacy of the Austin rule since it was issued by City Hall two days earlier and was not passed by a City Council vote.

November 1—A judge told Tennessee officials on Monday to stop enforcing new rules that have been used to arrest Occupy protesters in **Nashville**. State Attorney General's Office Senior Counsel Bill Marett announced at the beginning of a hearing before Judge Aleta Trauger that the state would not fight efforts to halt the policy. The judge said she had already decided to grant the restraining order because the curfew was a "clear prior restraint on free speech rights." Military veterans join the protesters at Zuccotti Park.

November 2—Demonstrations continued in **Oakland**, California, with a citywide general strike taking place in response to the serious injury sustained by a protester on October 25. **Protesters shut down the Port of Oakland**, the nation's fifth busiest port.

November 3—Riot police clashed with Occupy **Oakland**, firing tear gas and flash bang grenades. Over a hundred protesters were arrested, including another Iraq veteran who was seriously injured by police. Occupy **Seattle** protesters and police briefly clashed in protests sparked by Chase CEO Jamie Dimon's visit to town. Five protesters were arrested for breaking into the bank, and two police officers sustained minor injuries.

November 6—Global uprisings in **Egypt, Tunisia,** and **Iran.** With a population of just 430, **Mosier, Oregon** became the smallest U.S. town to have an active Occupy camp.

November 11—**International Day of Action.** Demonstrations took place in **Tunis** and **Cairo.** Occupy **Frankfurt** made a St. Martin's Day lantern march. One of the day's largest demonstrations happened in **Bologna** where students and occupiers demonstrated together. On New York City's Foley Square, Queen Mother Dr. Delois Blakely spoke, and Joan Baez sang for the protesters.

November 14—Occupy **Oakland** is cleared by police; twenty protesters are arrested. Oakland Mayor Jean Quan cited the eviction as a response to the "tremendous strain" the camp had put on the city's resources. The mayor's legal advisor, Dan Siegel, has resigned from his position in protest of the eviction.

November 15—

- **Occupy Wall Street** At about 1 a.m., NYPD began to clear Zuccotti Park.
- **Occupy D.C.** staged a sit-in at the DC headquarters of Brookview Properties, which administers New York City's Zuccotti Park.
- **Occupy UC Davis** held a rally on the campus, which was attended by approximately 2,000 people. Later, about 400 individuals occupied the Administration building and held a General Assembly in the space.
- **Occupy Cal** gathered over a thousand people at a rally at Sproul Hall plaza.
- **Occupy Seattle** rallied and marched downtown; police clashed with protesters, used pepper-spray, and arrested six.

November 16—Arrests took place in **Portland, Berkeley, San Francisco** (95 protesters arrested that night), **St. Louis** and **Los Angeles**.

November 17—**Day of Action** marking the two-month anniversary of the OWS movement.

- **Occupy Wall Street** saw crowds of more than 30,000 marching in the streets of New York City. Crowds assembled in and around Zuccotti Park, Union Square, Foley Square, the Brooklyn Bridge, and other locations through the city.
- **Occupy Portland**—Police in Portland used pepper spray on protesters there. At least 25 arrested on the Steel Bridge.
- **Occupy Los Angeles**—At least 30 were arrested. Protesters occupied Bank of America plaza.
- **Occupy Boston**—Judge issues a restraining order preventing police from evicting protesters.
- **Occupy Spokane**—Permit issued allowing protesters to camp.
- **Occupy Milwaukee**—Occupy protesters shut down the North Avenue Bridge.
- **Occupy Seattle** Occupy protesters marched on University Bridge, blocked traffic.
- **Occupy Dallas**—Camp evicted, 18 arrests.
- **Occupy Davis** and **Occupy UC Davis**—Students continued their occupation of the administration building and protesters erected tents on the campus quad.
- **Occupy Cal**—Students at UC Berkeley maintained their re-established encampment.

November 18—Police stage 2:00 a.m. raid at **Occupy Cal**. Campus police raid the **Occupy Davis** encampment in the morning, pepper-spraying multiple students with no provocation.

November 19—Former **Philadelphian** Police Captain Ray Lewis was arrested at Zuccotti Park. Protesters at the **University of California, Davis**, were pepper sprayed, prompting outrage. Also, **Occupy K St./DC** liberated the empty, city-owned Franklin School. In a move similar to other recent building occupations in **Oakland, Chapel Hill, New York,** and **London,** dozens of occupiers entered the building with sleeping bags and food and declared their intent to stay indefinitely.

November 22—Occupiers of **Tahrir Square** issued an urgent call for global solidarity, asking the world to: Occupy/shut-down **Egyptian** embassies worldwide; shut down the arms dealers; and shut down the part of your government dealing with the Egyptian junta. Hundreds marched on the Egyptian consulate in New York City.

November 25—Occupy **Seattle** joined with **Occupy Tacoma, Occupy Bellingham** and **Occupy Everett** in a statewide protest at Wal-Mart in Renton.

November 26—An **Egyptian** solidarity rally was held at the Egypt Mission (East 44th St & 2nd Ave) in Manhattan, with a march at 4 p.m.

November 27—Occupy **Philly** and **Occupy LA** were faced with eminent eviction.

Useful Contact Information

181st St Community Garden
beautificationproject.blogspot.com
212-543-9017
880 West 181st Street, #4B
New York, NY 10033

Ali Forney Center
www.aliforneycenter.org
212-222-3427
224 W. 35th St. Suite 1102
New York, NY 10001

ALIGN - the Alliance for a Greater New York
alignny.org
contact@alignny.org
212-631-0886
50 Broadway, 29th Floor, New York, NY 10004

ANSWER Coalition
answercoalition.org
nyc@internationalanswer.org
212- 694-8720
2295 Adam Clayton Powell Jr. Blvd., New York, NY 10030

Asian American Arts Centre
http://www.artspiral.org/

CAAAV
caav.org

Campaign to End the Death Penalty
www.nodeathpenalty.org

Campaign to End the New Jim Crow
endnewjimcrow.com

Center for Immigrant Families
212-531-3011
20 W 104th St
New York, NY 10025

Coalition for the Homeless
coalitionforthehomeless.org
info@cfthomeless.org
212-776-2000
129 Fulton Street, New York, NY 10038

Code Pink
codepinkalert.org
info@codepinkalert.org
310-827-4320

Community Voices Heard
cvhaction.org

Families for Freedom
familiesforfreedom.org
info@familiesforfreedom.org
3 West 29th St, #1030, New York, NY 10001
646 290 5551

FIERCE
www.fiercenyc.org
147 West 24th Street, 6th Floor, New York, NY 10011
646-336-6789

Fort Greene SNAP
fortgreenesnap.org

FUREE
furee.org
718-852-2960
81 Willoughby Street, 701, Brooklyn, NY 11201

Green Chimneys
www.greenchimneys.org
718-732-1501
79 Alexander Ave – 42A, Bronx, NY 10454

GOLES
info@goles.org
169 Avenue B, New York, NY 10009
212-358-1231

Guide to New York City Women's and Social Justice Organizations
bcrw.barnard.edu/guide

Immigrant Movement International
immigrant-movement.us
united@immigrant-movement.us
108-59 Roosevelt Avenue, Queens, NY 11368 USA

Industrial Workers of the World
iww.org/en
wobblycity.wordpress.com

International Socialist Organization
internationalsocialist.org
contact@internationalsocialist.org
773-583-5069
ISO National Office P.O. Box 16085 Chicago, IL 60616

Iraq Veterans Against the War
www.ivaw.org/new-york-city
646-723-0989
P.O. Box 3565 New York, NY 10008-3565

La Union
la-union.org

Labor community forum
laborcommunityforum@gmail.com

Make the Road
maketheroadny.org
Bushwick, Brooklyn: 301 Grove Street Brooklyn, New York 11237
718-418-7690
Jackson Heights, Queens: 92-10 Roosevelt Avenue,
Jackson Heights, New York 11372
718-565-8500
Port Richmond, Staten Island:479 Port Richmond Avenue,
Staten Island, New York 10302
718-727-1222

Malcom X Grassroots Movement
mxgm.org
718-254-8800
PO BOX 471711 Brooklyn, NY 11247

Marriage Equality NY (MENY)
www.meny.us

Mirabal Sisters Community and Cultural Center
Mirabalcenter.org
info@mirabalcenter.org
212-234-3002

National Lawyers Guild
www.nlg.org
nlgnyc.org
212-679-5100
132 Nassau Street, Rm. 922, New York, NY 10038

New York Collective of Radical Educators (NYCORE)
nycore.org

New York Students Rising
nystudentsrising.org

NMASS
nmass.org
nmass@nmass.org

No Gas Pipeline
nogaspipeline.org
nogaspipeline@gmail.com
235 3rd Street, Jersey City, NJ 07302

Northwest Bronx Community and Clergy Coalition
northwestbronx.org
718-584-0515
103 East 196th Street Bronx, NY 10468

NYU4OWS
nyu4ows.tumblr.com

Occupy the DOE
nycore.org/occupy-the-doe/

Occupy Equality NY
www.facebook.com/groups/OccupyEqualityNY/

Occupy Wall Street
www.occupywallst.org/
General Inquiries: general@occupywallst.org
+1 (516) 708-4777

Organizing for Occupation
www.o4onyc.org

Parent Occupy Wall St
parents@everythingindependent.com

Parents for Occupy Wall Street
parentsforoccupywallst.com

Picture the Homeless
picturethehomeless.org
info@picturethehomeless.org

Queer Rising
QueerRising.org
queerrising@gmail.com
917-520-8554

Queerocracy
www.queerocracy.org
contact@queerocracy.org

Shut Down Indian Point Now
shutdownindianpointnow.org

Speak Up HP
speakuphp.org
info@speakuphp.org

Strong Economy for All Coalition
strongforall.org/coalition

Students United for a Free CUNY
studentsunitedforafreecuny.wordpress.com

Writers for the 99%

A.J. Bauer, Christine Baumgarthuber, Jed Bickman, Jeremy Brecher, Morgan Buck, Ana M. Chavez, Suzanne Collado, Sharon Cooper, Jackie DiSalvo, Robin Epstein, Liza Featherstone, Sean Firko, Claudia Sofía Garriga López, Alejandro Gomez-del-Moral, Kate Griffiths-Dingani, Katherine Gressel, Alex Hall, Samantha Hammer, Malcolm Harris, Zoe Heller, Travis Holloway, Rana Jaleel, Vani Kannan, Danny Katch, Zenia Kish, Sean Larson, Kathryn L. Mahaney, Brian Merchant, Lisa Montanarelli, Debbie Nathan, Angelique V. Nixon, David Osborn, Willie Osterweil, Amity Paye, Jon L Peacock, Justin Owen Rawlins, Colin Robinson, Olivia Rosane, James Frederic Rose, Andrew Ross, Koren Shadmi, Benjamin Shepard, Christine Utz, Danny Valdez, Susan Wilcox, Jamie Yancovitz.